LONGMAN

CORNERSTONE

C

Anna Uhl Chamot

Jim Cummins

Sharroky Hollie

PEARSON
Longman

Longman Cornerstone C

Pearson Education, 10 Bank Street, White Plains, NY 10606

Staff credits: The people who made up the *Longman Cornerstone* team, representing editorial, production, design, manufacturing, and marketing, are John Ade, Rhea Banker, Liz Barker, Don Bensey, Kenna Bourke, Jeffrey Buckner, Brandon Carda, Daniel Comstock, Gina DiLillo, Johnnie Farmer, Patrice Fraccio, Zach Halper, Sarah Hughes, Ed Lamprich, Niki Lee, Christopher Leonowicz, Linda Moser, Micheal O'Loughlin, Liza Pleva, Edie Pullman, Tara Rose, Tania Saiz-Sousa, Loretta Steeves, Andrew Vaccaro

Text design and composition: The Quarasan Group, Inc.
Illustration and photo credits: See page 361.

Library of Congress Cataloging-in-Publication Data
Chamot, Anna Uhl.
   Longman cornerstone / Anna Uhl Chamot, Jim Cummins, Sharroky Hollie.
   p. cm. - - (Longman cornerstone; C)
   Includes index.
   1. Language arts (Elementary school)—United States. 2. Language arts
(Elementary school)—Activity programs 3. English language—Study and teaching.
   I. Cummins, Jim II. Hollie, Sharroky III. Title.

ISBN-13: 978-0-13-504803-0
ISBN-10: 0-13-504803-6

PEARSON LONGMAN ON THE WEB

Pearsonlongman.com offers online resources for teachers and students. Access our Companion Websites, our online catalog, and our local offices around the world.

Visit us at **www.pearsonlongman.com**.

Printed in the United States of America

4 5 6 7 8 9 10–CRK–12 11 10 09

About the Authors

Anna Uhl Chamot is a professor of secondary education and a faculty advisor for ESL in George Washington University's Department of Teacher Preparation. She has been a researcher and teacher trainer in content-based, second-language learning and language-learning strategies. She co-designed and has written extensively about the Cognitive Academic Language Learning Approach (CALLA) and spent seven years implementing the CALLA model in the Arlington Public Schools in Virginia.

Jim Cummins is the Canada Research Chair in the Department of Curriculum, Teaching, and Learning of the Ontario Institute for Studies in Education at the University of Toronto. His research focuses on literacy development in multilingual school contexts, as well as on the potential roles of technology in promoting language and literacy development. His recent publications include: *The International Handbook of English Language Teaching* (co-edited with Chris Davison) and *Literacy, Technology, and Diversity: Teaching for Success in Changing Times* (with Kristin Brown and Dennis Sayers).

Sharroky Hollie is an assistant professor in teacher education at California State University, Dominguez Hills. His expertise is in the field of professional development, African-American education, and second-language methodology. He is an urban literacy visiting professor at Webster University, St. Louis. Sharroky is the Executive Director of the Center for Culturally Responsive Teaching and Learning (CCRTL) and the co-founding director of the nationally-acclaimed Culture and Language Academy of Success (CLAS).

Consultants and Reviewers

Rebecca Anselmo
Sunrise Acres Elementary School
Las Vegas, NV

Ana Applegate
Redlands School District
Redlands, CA

Terri Armstrong
Houston ISD
Houston, TX

Jacqueline Avritt
Riverside County Office of Ed.
Hemet, CA

Mitchell Bobrick
Palm Beach County School
West Palm Beach, FL

Victoria Brioso-Saldala
Broward County Schools
Fort Lauderdale, FL

Brenda Cabarga Schubert
Creekside Elementary School
Salinas, CA

Joshua Ezekiel
Bardin Elementary School
Salinas, CA

Veneshia Gonzalez
Seminole Elementary School
Okeechobee, FL

Carolyn Grigsby
San Francisco Unified School District
San Francisco, CA

Julie Grubbe
Plainfield Consolidated Schools
Chicago, IL

Yasmin Hernandez-Manno
Newark Public Schools
Newark, NJ

Janina Kusielewicz
Clifton Public Schools/Bilingual Ed.
& Basic Skills Instruction Dept.
Clifton, NJ

Mary Helen Lechuga
El Paso ISD
El Paso, TX

Gayle P. Malloy
Randolph School District
Randolph, MA

Randy Payne
Patterson/Taft Elementaries
Mesa, AZ

Marcie L. Schnegelberger
Alisal Union SD
Salinas, CA

Lorraine Smith
Collier County Schools
Naples, FL

Shawna Stoltenborg
Glendale Elementary School
Glen Burnie, MD

Denise Tiffany
West High School
Iowa City, IO

Dear Student,

Welcome to *Longman Cornerstone!*

We wrote *Longman Cornerstone* to help you succeed in all your school studies. This program will help you learn the English language you need to study language arts, social studies, math, and science. You will learn how to speak to family members, classmates, and teachers in English.

Cornerstone includes a mix of many subjects. Each unit has four different readings that include some fiction (made-up) and nonfiction (true) articles, stories, songs, and poems. The readings will give you some of the tools you need to do well in all your subjects in school.

As you use this program, you will build on what you already know, learn new words, new information and facts, and take part in creative activities. The activities will help you improve your English skills.

Learning a language takes time, but just like learning to skateboard or learning to swim, it is fun!

We hope you enjoy *Longman Cornerstone* as much as we enjoyed writing it for you!

Good luck!

Anna Uhl Chamot
Jim Cummins
Sharroky Hollie

Your *Cornerstone* Unit!

Cornerstones are important for a building and important for learning, too.

Meet the program that will give you the cornerstones you need to improve in English and do better in all your subjects in school.

Kick Off Each Unit

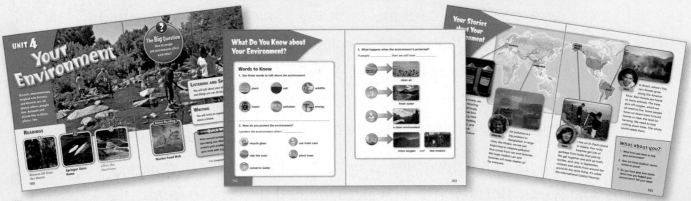

? Big Question

The Big Question pulls all the readings together and helps you focus on big ideas.

Words to Know

Learn new vocabulary for the unit theme.

Mini-Autobiographies

Meet other students and hear what they say about the unit theme.

For Each Reading

Vocabulary

Get to know the words *before* you read.

Readings ❶, ❷, and ❸

Read with success! Get help from glossed words and Check-Up questions.

After Each Reading

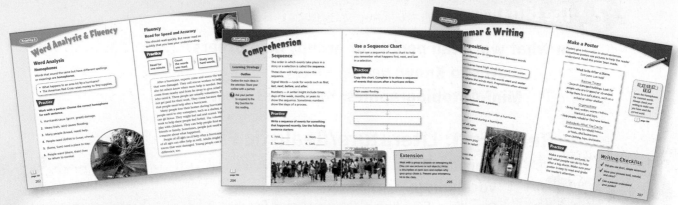

Word Analysis & Fluency
Become a better reader by learning about phonics and how words are formed. Then practice reading with ease on the fluency pages.

Comprehension
Focus on a comprehension skill and practice it using a graphic organizer.

Grammar & Writing
Learn rules of grammar to help you communicate. Then improve your writing skills.

Wrap Up Each Unit

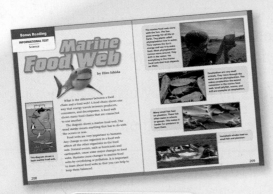

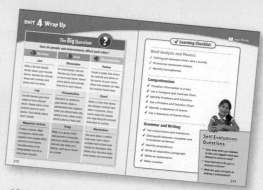

Bonus Reading
Take a break and read for fun.

? Wrap up
Discuss the Big Question with your class. Choose an Assessment Project to show all you have learned.

UNIT 1

Helping Others

Heroes and Their Journeys

? The **Big** Question

Building a New Country

? The Big Question

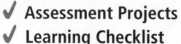

Your Environment

? The **Big** Question

UNIT 5 Contents

Sounds and Music

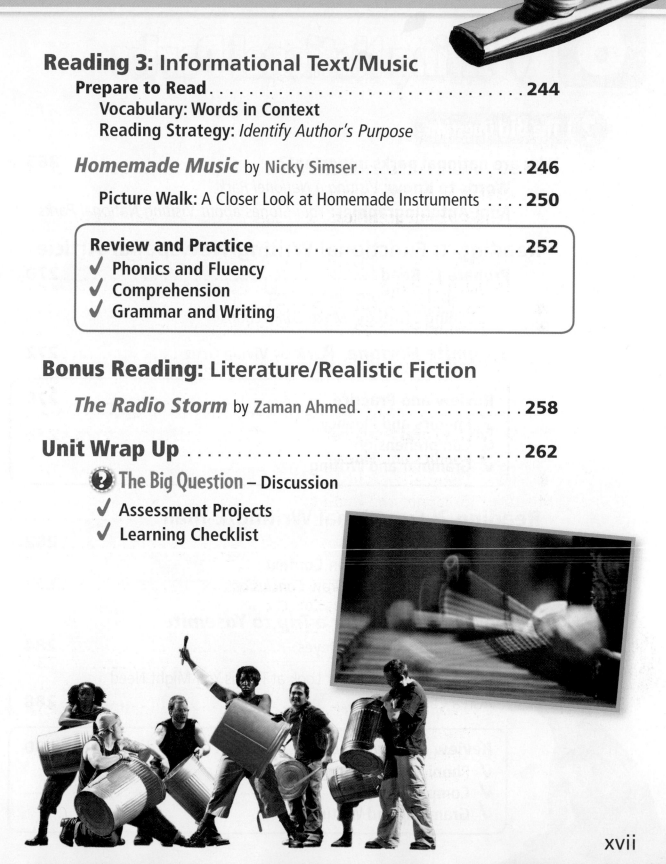

UNIT 6

Contents

Visiting National Parks

? The Big Question

Reading 1: Functional Writing/Newspaper Article

Reading 2: Functional Writing/E-mail

UNIT 1
Helping Others

Teamwork can be hard sometimes, but when everyone pitches in, the results can be amazing.

READINGS

Everybody Wins

Doctors Without Borders

Stone Soup

2

The Big Question

In what ways can people or groups help others?

LISTENING AND SPEAKING

You will tell a story about people helping each other.

WRITING

You will write a story about a problem you had to solve.

Quick Write

What does cooperation mean to you? Write several sentences to explain your ideas.

Bonus Reading

A Team Crosses the Finish Line

What Do You Know about Helping Others?

Words to Know

1. Use these words to talk about people you can help.

In my family, I help my _parents_ .

 grandmother

 aunt

 cousin

 grandfather

 uncle

 parents

---

2. What chores do you do at home?

In my home, I _____ .

 set the table

 make my bed

 vacuum

 take out the garbage

 sweep

 run errands

3. How do you help?

When I _get supplies_ , I _recycle_ .

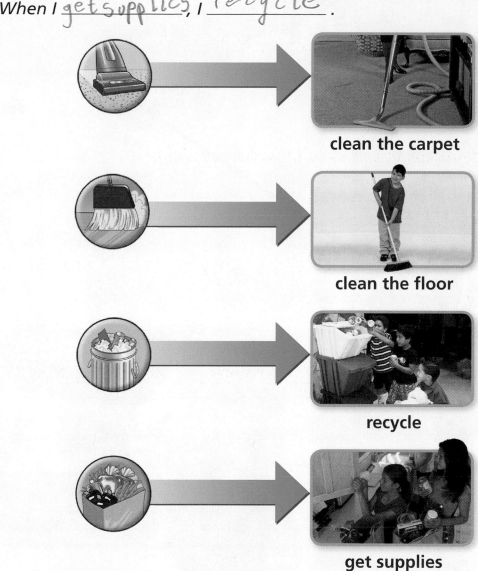

clean the carpet

clean the floor

recycle

get supplies

4. Use these words to talk about people who can help you.

physician **crossing guard** **firefighter** **instructor**

Your Stories about Helping

Ohio, U.S.A.

Spain

Charlie

In my town in Ohio, we celebrate the Fourth of July every year with a potluck picnic. Every family brings a different dish, and we all share each other's food. There is always plenty of food to eat. We have a lot of fun.

Clara

I live in Spain. There was a huge oil spill a few years ago. The beaches were full of oil sludge. Many birds were covered with oil and were dying. People from all over the world came to help clean up after the oil spill.

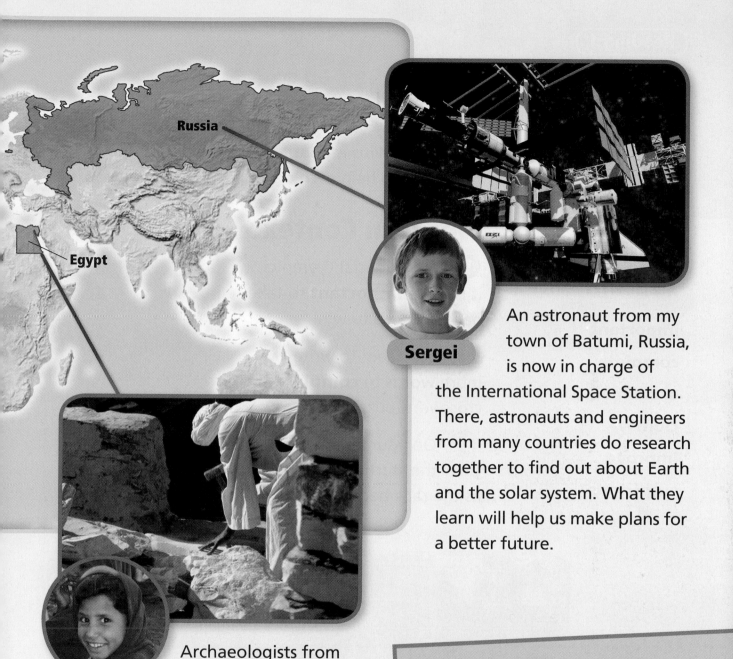

Russia

Egypt

Sergei

An astronaut from my town of Batumi, Russia, is now in charge of the International Space Station. There, astronauts and engineers from many countries do research together to find out about Earth and the solar system. What they learn will help us make plans for a better future.

Mert

Archaeologists from all over the world have come to Egypt to participate in archaeological digs in the Valley of the Kings. A team of experts working together uncovered a tomb near the tomb of King Tutankhamen. By helping each other, experts learn more about ancient history.

What about you?

1 When have you worked with others?

2 How are these students' stories similar to yours?

3 Do you have a story about people helping each other? Tell your story!

Everybody Wins

Vocabulary

Everybody Wins is about two teammates who find ways to help each other.

Key Words

- **important**
- **complete**
- **exclaimed**
- **clumsy**
- **improve**
- **suspicious**

Words in Context

1 In the Special Olympics, it is more **important** to take part than it is to win.

2 Lucy needs to write two more words to **complete** the crossword puzzle.

3 "On your mark. Get set. Go!" the starter **exclaimed** as the race began.

④ Even the best servers are sometimes **clumsy**.

⑤ My grandparents started working out at the gym twice a week in order to **improve** their health.

⑥ Mrs. Jones was **suspicious** when we turned in our homework. Everybody had the same answers.

Practice

Use each key word in a sentence.

Make Connections

Everybody Wins is about how two girls who have different problems learn to work together. Has this ever happened to you? Tell your story to a partner.

Academic Words

conduct
lead or direct

project
plan or activity

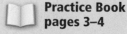 Practice Book
pages 3–4

LITERATURE

Realistic Fiction

The **Big** Question

How can people who are good at different things help each other?

Reading Strategy

Preview and Predict

- Read the title.
- Look at the illustrations.
- Read the words and the definitions at the bottom of each page.
- Read the first and last paragraph of the story.
- Predict what the story will be about.

Everybody Wins

by Pamela Walker
illustrated by Meredith Johnson

Casey was the best basketball player on the school team. She made more baskets than anyone else. She would dribble the ball past her teammates to the basket. Some of the other girls on the team called her a ball hog.

"Why didn't you pass the ball to Jessie?" Damaris asked after a game. "She was right under the basket."

"Because Jessie's too clumsy!" Casey exclaimed. "I wanted to win."

Carla said, "You're being mean. Jessie tries really hard. Besides, we're a team."

Winning was more important to Casey than working with her team.

---

dribble   move a ball forward by bouncing it

ball hog   someone who will not give the ball to other players on the team

pass   throw

The next day, Mr. Vega asked to speak to Casey after class. He told Casey she got another low score on her science test.

"You're going to have to do much better," Mr. Vega said. "Unless your grades improve, you will have to quit the team."

"Quit the team!" Casey cried. "But I have to play basketball!"

"I'm sorry," Mr. Vega said. "These are the rules. You have three weeks to improve your science grade."

Casey couldn't believe what she was hearing! She would do anything to keep from being kicked off the team.

"Maybe you should ask Jessie to help you," Mr. Vega said. "She's one of my best science students."

CheckUp How do you think Casey will react to Mr. Vega's idea?

Casey was angry. The team's most important game of the year was in three weeks. She couldn't miss it. How could Mr. Vega be so mean? He knew the team wouldn't win if she didn't play.

Casey ran out of Mr. Vega's classroom. She did not look where she was going, and she crashed into Damaris and Carla.

"What's the matter?" asked Damaris.

"Mr. Vega said I am failing science. He said I can't play basketball if I don't get better grades," Casey said.

"Why don't you ask Jessie to help you?" asked Damaris.

"She's really good at science," said Carla.

"But she's angry with me," said Casey.

---

angry   not happy

failing   not doing well

Jessie came out of the art room as the other girls were talking.

"Hey, Jessie!" Carla said. "Casey wants to ask you something."

"I need your help," said Casey.

Jessie was puzzled. "Why should I help you?" she asked.

"I'm sorry I was mean to you. But, if you help me with science, I'll help you with basketball," said Casey.

"Why?" asked Jessie.

"Because if I don't do better in science class, I will be off the basketball team," Casey said.

"Come on," said Damaris. "You two can help each other. Everybody will win."

"It's worth a try," said Carla. "Okay?"

"Okay," said Jessie. "We can try to help each other."

Check Up ▸ Do you think the girls' plan will work? Why?

For the next three weeks, Jessie helped Casey with her science homework.

"When you study," Jessie told Casey, "first read the chapter all the way through. Then go back and write down the words you don't know. You can look up these words in the dictionary."

Jessie even made a practice science quiz for Casey to complete.

During basketball practice, Casey began to pass the ball to Jessie. At first the other girls were suspicious. Why was Casey being so helpful?

"Don't forget to bend your knees right before you shoot," Casey told Jessie during practice.

Casey's science grade improved, and she stayed on the team. Jessie began to improve in basketball, too.

Near the end of the next big game, Casey had the ball. The crowd was yelling and screaming. She was starting to dribble the ball toward the basket when she saw Jessie wave to her.

Jessie was wide open and right under the basket.

Casey passed the ball to her, and Jessie shot it into the basket!

"Great job, Jessie!" the team exclaimed. "We won! We won!"

"We won because Casey helped me," said Jessie.

"Great job, Casey!" the team said.

"No," said Casey. "We won because we're a team."

The girls laughed. "Great job, team!"

In the huddle after the game, the team shouted, "Everybody wins!"

---

wide open   standing with nobody in the way

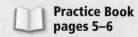

Practice Book
pages 5–6

Reading Strategy

Preview and Predict

Before you read the story, you previewed it and made predictions.

- Were your predictions correct?
- Did making predictions help you to understand the story? How?

Think It Over

1 Who asks Jessie to help Casey?

2 How do Casey and Jessie help each other?

3 What have Casey and Jessie learned by the end of the story?

Phonics & Fluency

Phonics

Short Vowels

The letters *a*, *e*, *i*, *o*, and *u* are **vowels**.
Each word in the chart has one vowel.

Short Vowels				
a	e	i	o	u
am	Ed	if	on	up
can	get	win	job	but

Rule Box

When a word has a single vowel, the vowel sound is usually short.

Practice

Read the sentences with a partner. Look for short vowels.

- Will you let me join the team?
- Did you make the cut?
- Here is the game plan.
- Take your best shot.
- It's a <u>slam</u> <u>dunk</u>.

1. Make a short vowel chart like the one above.

2. Add the short vowel words you found to the chart.

3. Add one more word for each short vowel.

Practice
Book

page 7

16

Fluency

Look Ahead

Sometimes readers look for hard words before they read. They then try to figure them out.

Practice

| Pick one passage. | → | Find any hard words. | → | Practice saying those words. | → | Read the passage aloud. |

1. Casey was the best basketball player on the team. Jessie was an average player on the team. One day, they found out that they could both win if they learned to help each other.

2. Casey was the best basketball player on the school team. She made more baskets than anyone else. She would dribble the ball past her teammates to the basket. Some of the other girls on the team called her a ball hog.

3. "When you study," Jessie told Casey, "first read the chapter all the way through. Then go back and write down the words you don't know. You can look up these words in the dictionary."

   Jessie even made a practice science quiz for Casey to complete.

Comprehension

Learning Strategy

Retell

Retell the story to a partner.

 Ask your partner to respond to the Big Question for this reading.

Preview and Predict

After previewing, you can predict what you think the story will be about.

Practice

Answer the questions.

1. What did you learn from previewing the story?

2. What did you predict the story was about? Were you right?

3. The reading that starts on page 24 is nonfiction. What additional text features might you check as you preview the text?

4. Preview the next reading. What do you think it will be about?

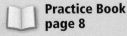
Practice Book page 8

Use a Problem and Solution Chart

Writers often use problems and solutions in stories. Identifying the problems and solutions will help you better understand the story.

Practice

Copy this Problem and Solution Chart. Complete it to show each problem and solution from the story. Share your work with a partner.

Problem	Solution
The Team's Problem: Casey was not letting other players have the ball.	
Casey's Problem:	
Jessie's Problem:	

Extension

Talk with your partner about things that each of you is good at. How could you use those skills to help each other? Present your ideas to the class using a visual aid.

Grammar & Writing

Singular and Plural Nouns

Singular nouns name one person, place, or thing. The words *team*, *basket*, and *game* are singular nouns. **Plural** nouns name more than one person, place, or thing. The words *players*, *teammates,* and *rules* are plural nouns.

Rule Box

To form the plural of most words, you simply add the letter **s**. To form the plural of nouns that end in *s*, *ss*, *ch*, *sh*, or *x*, you add **-es**. You form the plural of nouns that end in a consonant and *y* by changing the *y* to i and adding **-es**.

Practice

Copy each singular noun. Write the plural form.

1. month   **3.** box   **5.** game

2. class   **4.** sandwich   **6.** party

Practice Book
page 9

20

Write a Narrative

When you write a **narrative**, you tell details about an event that happened. Sometimes writers use the 5W questions to help see if they have included all the details in their narrative. The 5W question words are: *who*, *what*, *where*, *when*, and *why*.

Read about Pedro's trip to a NASCAR race.

I love cars! My father took me to a NASCAR race in Daytona because I got straight A's on my report card. It was so exciting! I was amazed at all the colorful cars and the large crowd. The crowd started to scream as the race was about to begin. Then the starting flag came down, and the cars zoomed around the track. There was even a crash. Luckily, nobody was hurt. The cars went around the track many, many times. Finally, my favorite driver came in first. It was a great day!

SPELLING TIP

If you are not sure of the spelling of a word, use a dictionary to check the spelling.

Practice Book page 10

Practice

Write a paragraph about a sporting event you attended. If you have not been to one, you can make it up!

- Tell which sporting event you attended.
- Add enough details to explain what happened.
- Be sure to answer the 5W questions.

Writing Checklist

✔ Did you use singular and plural nouns correctly?

✔ Did you answer the 5W questions?

✔ Can a partner understand your paragraph?

Doctors Without Borders

Vocabulary

Doctors Without Borders is about an organization that sends doctors to help people in need all over the world.

Words in Context

Key Words

- emergency
- courageous
- teamwork
- training
- intervene
- refugees

1 These operators answer the telephone when people call 911 to report an **emergency**.

2 Firefighters have to be **courageous**. They put their lives in danger so that we can be safe. They often work together to put out a fire. That is real **teamwork**.

③ The local community center offers **training** to show people how to care for others who are sick or hurt.

④ Sometimes an adult has to **intervene** when students have problems.

⑤ **Refugees** are people who have to leave their countries because of war or food shortages.

Practice

Use each key word in a sentence.

Make Connections

Suppose you were asked to help others in another country. What help would you like to give? What supplies would you need to bring with you?

Academic Words

evaluate

look at something carefully

___

task

job to be done

 Practice Book pages 11–12

The Big Question

Why do volunteers help people in other countries?

Reading Strategy

Activate Prior Knowledge

Before you read, ask yourself:

- What do I already know about doctors?
- What do I want to find out about Doctors Without Borders?
- Copy the chart on page 33. Fill in the first two columns.

Doctors Without Borders

by Douglas Weisser

When we are sick or hurt, we go to the doctor. Some places in the world do not have enough doctors or supplies to help people. This is really true when there is a crisis in that place.

A group called Doctors Without Borders works to help people in need. If there is an emergency, these doctors volunteer to go where they are needed. The group gives medical care and other services. Doctors Without Borders has been helping people since 1971.

---

supplies   things that people want or need

A member of Doctors Without Borders with refugees in Ethiopia.

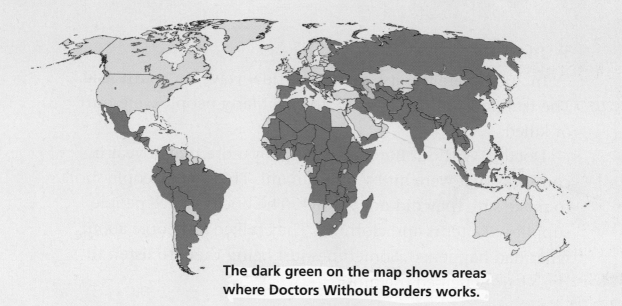

The dark green on the map shows areas where Doctors Without Borders works.

Bringing Help Where It Is Needed

The doctors bring their medical skills to places where they are needed. They also bring supplies like blankets and drinking water. Sometimes the doctors train other people so they can help, too.

This doctor helped a child in Sri Lanka.

Doctors Without Borders has worked in countries all over the world. If there is a war in a country, the people there need help. Refugees are people who have to leave their homes. They leave because there is no food or because fighting has made their homes unsafe.

Doctors Without Borders can intervene to help refugees. Sometimes, refugees do not even have clean water. The volunteers come with water and medicine. They teach refugees how to eat better and stay healthy. They can show refugees how to make water safe for drinking.

---

skills   something a person does well

medicine   a substance used to treat sickness

healthy   not sick

Check Up Where might Doctors Without Borders have gone recently to help?

25

Tsunami!

In 2004 there was a tsunami, or tidal wave, in South Asia. The tsunami destroyed many towns. Many people were hurt or killed.

Doctors Without Borders worked for more than a year in countries that were hit by the tsunami. They gave people shots to make sure they did not get sick. The doctors gave people supplies like tents and clothing. They talked to people about what had happened. Sometimes just being there to listen to the victims helped the most.

---

tsunami   huge wave that causes great destruction on land

destroyed   damaged so that it cannot be used

victims   people who have been affected by something bad

Workers unload supplies that doctors used to help the 2004 tsunami victims.

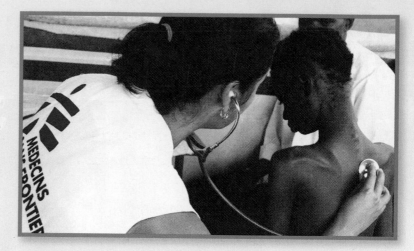

A doctor helps a boy in Sri Lanka after the 2004 tsunami.

Helping Others Help Themselves

Sometimes the volunteers help people in a town build new hospitals. That involves real teamwork!

Sometimes the best help the volunteers can give is training. It can be better for Doctors Without Borders to help train local doctors to take care of people after a crisis. The local doctors can give care to sick and hurt people after Doctors Without Borders leaves the area.

The volunteers who work for Doctors Without Borders travel all over the world to help people after emergencies. They are courageous, and borders do not stop them.

Practice Book pages 13–14

Reading Strategy

Activate Prior Knowledge

- How did your knowledge of doctors help you understand the reading?
- What have you learned about Doctors Without Borders?
- What else would you like to learn?

Think It Over

1 What is Doctors Without Borders?

2 How does Doctors Without Borders help people?

3 How did Doctors Without Borders help people after the tsunami in South Asia?

27

Doctors Without Borders

▲ **Angola**
Doctors Without Borders sets up centers to feed people who are hungry.

▲ **Tibet**
Doctors Without Borders works to help people in rural Tibet get clean drinking water.

▲ **Afghanistan**
This volunteer is training women in Afghanistan to provide care for the people in their village.

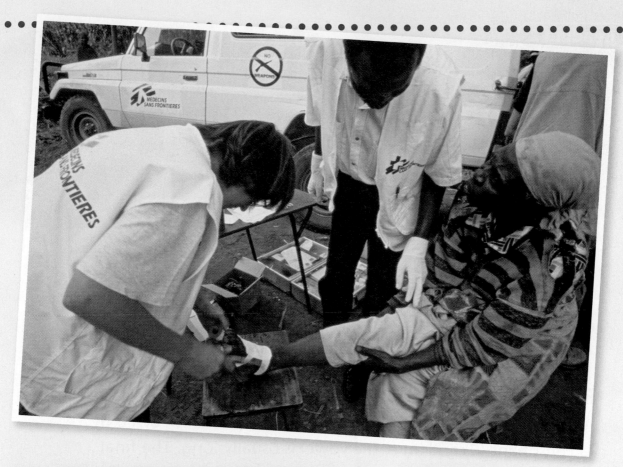

▲ Rwanda

These volunteers are taking care of a refugee's injured leg.

▲ Kenya

This doctor is giving a woman and her child checkups.

Activity to Do!

These pages use pictures and words to tell where Doctors Without Borders works.

- Research any country that interests you.

- Create two pages, using pictures and words, to tell about that country.

Phonics & Fluency

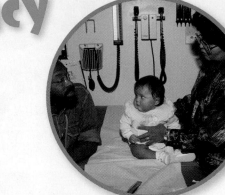

Phonics

Long Vowels with Silent e

Read the words on the chart. Which vowels say their names?

a_e	i_e	o_e	u_e
age	ice	woke	use
take	fine	globe	cube

Rule Box

When the first vowel (**V**) in a one-syllable word is followed by a consonant (**C**) and an **e**, the vowel is usually long. The final **e** is silent. This is the "silent **e** rule."

Some words that have a *v*, *m*, or *n* after the first vowel are exceptions to the rule.

Practice

With a partner, take turns reading the words below.

1. Use the words to make two lists.

   • Words that follow the silent *e* rule.
   • Exceptions to the silent *e* rule.

2. Read your list of words that follow the silent *e* rule to your partner. Point to and say the name of the long vowel in each word.

like	safe
gave	give
ate	line
gone	plane
make	move

Practice Book

page 15

Fluency

Read for Speed and Accuracy

You should read quickly. But never read so quickly that you lose your understanding.

Practice

| Read for one minute. | Count the words you read. | Study any hard words. | Read and count again. |

When we are sick or hurt, we go to the doctor. Some places	13
in the world do not have enough doctors or supplies to help	25
people. This is really true when there is a crisis in that place.	38
A group called Doctors Without Borders works to help	47
people in need. If there is an emergency, these doctors	57
volunteer to go where they are needed. The group gives	67
medical care and other services. Doctors Without Borders	75
has been helping people since 1971.	81
The doctors bring their medical skills to places where	90
they are needed. They also bring supplies like blankets and	100
drinking water. Sometimes the doctors train other people so	109
that they can help, too.	113

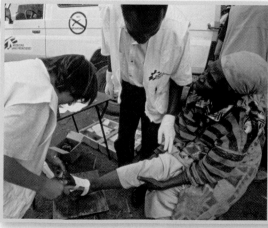

Comprehension

Activate Prior Knowledge

When you **activate prior knowledge**, you use what you already know to learn more about something. For example, you can use what you already know about doctors to learn more about what doctors do in *Doctors Without Borders.*

Practice

Imagine that your next reading assignment is about tsunamis.

1. List three things you already know about tsunamis based on what you read in *Doctors Without Borders.*

2. List three things you want to learn about tsunamis.

Use a KWL Chart

A KWL Chart can be used to activate prior knowledge. It provides a plan for recording three kinds of information.

1. What you **know** about a topic before reading.

2. What you **want** to learn about the topic.

3. What you actually **learned** about the topic.

Practice

You completed the first two columns before. Now complete the final column. Reread the selection for facts to add.

Topic: Doctors Without Borders		
What I Know	**What I Want to Know**	**What I Learned**

1. What do you still want to learn about Doctors Without Borders?

2. Where can you look to find more information?

Extension

Imagine that your teacher asked you to be a volunteer in your community. What kind of work would you like to do? Discuss your ideas with a partner. Then present them to the class using a visual aid.

33

Grammar & Writing

Past Tense Verbs

Verbs are words that name actions.

Past tense verbs name actions that already happened.

> The tsunami **destroyed** many towns.
>
> Doctors Without Borders **worked** in countries hit by the tsunami.

Rule Box

To form the past tense of most verbs, add *-ed, -d,* or *-ied* to the end of the word.

destroy → destroyed   save → saved   hurry → hurried

For words ending in a consonant, double the consonant and add *-ed.*

stop → stopped

Irregular verbs do not follow these rules. *Give, teach,* and *bring* are examples of irregular verbs. Their past tense forms are *gave, taught,* and *brought*.

Practice

Copy each verb. Write the past tense form.

1. need   3. decide   5. rub   7. treat

2. step   4. carry   6. place   8. dry

Practice Book page 17

Write a Paragraph with a Topic Sentence

A **paragraph** is a group of sentences that have the same topic or idea. One sentence, called the **topic sentence,** gives the main idea of the paragraph. The other sentences are related to the topic sentence. They give more information about the main idea.

Read this paragraph about how Donna solved a problem.

SPELLING TIP

To form the plural of most nouns, just add an -s.

📖 **Practice Book page 18**

I had a math test the following day, but I left my textbook at school. How was I going to study for the test? I was going out of my mind! My older brother saw that I was worried and decided to help me. He found his fifth grade math notes and made up math problems for me to practice. I was so ready for the test that I got an A!

Practice

Think about a problem that you had to solve. Write a paragraph about it.

- Start with a topic sentence that explains the problem.
- Add sentences to explain how you solved the problem.

Writing Checklist

✓ Did you write a clear topic sentence?

✓ Did you spell past tense verbs correctly?

✓ Can a partner understand both the problem and the solution?

Stone Soup

Vocabulary

Stone Soup is about a boy who finds a clever way to feed some hungry villagers.

Words in Context

1 I helped Mom and Dad **carry** the groceries when we got back from the store.

2 When it gets cold in the winter, flowers growing outside become **scarce**.

3 It's always nice to **share**!

Key Words

carry

scarce

share

peeked

cottage

charge

4 Jeffrey **peeked** out of the window to see if his mom's car was in the street.

5 The **cottage** was small but very cozy.

6 The elephants **charge** the lions at the watering hole.

Practice

Use each key word in a sentence.

Make Connections

The next story shows how everyone wins when people share. Do you have a story about sharing? Tell your story to a partner.

Practice Book
pages 19–20

Academic Words

attitude
point of view; state of mind

item
single thing or piece

LITERATURE

Folktale

The Big Question

What are the pros and cons of sharing?

Reading Strategy

Identify Events in a Plot

- Can you tell what happens first, next, and last in the story?
- How do you think the story ends?

Stone Soup

by P. J. Perkins
illustrated by Julie Downing

One of John's favorite things was a big iron pot. The pot had once belonged to his mother.

As much as he loved the pot, John was hungry. He decided to trade the pot for something to eat.

"I'm sorry," said the farmer's wife from her cottage door. "Food is scarce these days. I only have enough for my own family."

"Thank you, anyway," John said. "I will carry my pot to the next village."

John walked many miles.

"May I trade this nice iron pot for something to eat?" he asked everyone he saw.

But the people in this village were just as poor and hungry as John was.

---

belonged was owned

trade to give away for something else

village small town

As John started to leave the village, he saw a smooth, round stone in the road. If only this stone were something good to eat, he thought.

Then John got an idea. He filled his iron pot with water. He gathered sticks and dry wood and then built a blazing fire all around his pot.

As he waited for the water to get hot, he thought about how good his soup would taste. "This stone soup will be delicious!" he said to himself. "I can hardly wait to eat every drop!"

When the water began to bubble and boil, he dropped the stone into the pot.

---

gathered   collected

blazing   very bright

delicious   tastes or smells very good

Check Up   What event is happening on this page?

"What are you doing?" asked a little girl, who had been watching him from a nearby garden.

"I'm making stone soup," John told her.

"Stone soup!" she cried. "Is it good?"

"You've never had stone soup?" he asked. "Stone soup is delicious!"

The little girl peeked into the pot of water. She saw the stone at the bottom of the pot.

"I have some extra potatoes," she told him. "Would potatoes be good in stone soup?"

"I like stone soup just as it is," John said. "But I think potatoes will make it even better."

The little girl smiled. "Let's put them in!" she said as she dropped the potatoes into the boiling water.

---

garden   place where people grow fruit, vegetables, and flowers

As the potatoes began to cook, wonderful smells floated through the village from cottage to cottage.

A young boy came over with some carrots. "Your soup smells so good," the boy said. "Would these carrots be good in the soup?"

"This stone soup will be delicious," John told him. "But carrots will make it even better."

The boy dropped the carrots into the pot.

John sniffed the delicious aroma coming from the pot. "This will be the best stone soup ever," he said to the boy and girl.

That's when John saw how hungry the children looked.

"Will you stay and share this soup with me?" he asked them.

"Will there be enough?" the little girl asked.

"More than enough!" John said.

---

floated   traveled over air or water

aroma   odor

Check Up → What event happened on this page?

Soon, other people in the village began to charge toward John and his pot of stone soup.

"I've never heard of stone soup, but here is some meat," said a woman. "You may use it if you think it will be good in the soup."

"I have some onions," said another woman as she dropped them into the pot.

As the stone soup simmered, more and more people lined up to add something good to the pot.

John said to each person, "Please bring a bowl and spoon and share this soup with me. This is too much soup for me to eat alone."

Each person hurried home to get a bowl and spoon.

---

simmered cooked slowly

lined up stood one behind the other

When the soup had cooked, John looked at all the people who had gathered. Each person stood by the pot with a bowl and spoon. He wondered if there would be enough soup for everyone.

John looked into the pot of soup and saw the potatoes, carrots, onions, meat, and other good things. The pot was full!

John spooned the soup into everyone's bowls.

"This is the best soup ever!" exclaimed one person.

"I didn't know that stone soup could be so delicious!" said someone else.

After John finished his third bowl of soup, he called to the little girl who had given him potatoes. "This stone is for you," he said to her. "Now your village will never be hungry again."

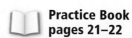

Practice Book pages 21–22

Reading Strategy

Identify Events in a Plot

- What happened in the beginning of the story?
- How did the story end?
- Can you think of another ending to the story?

Think It Over

1 What is John's problem?

2 What event gives John his big idea?

3 How do the villagers react when they smell the soup?

4 What does John give the little girl at the end?

Word Analysis & Fluency

Word Analysis

Multiple-Meaning Words

Some words have more than one meaning.

> John could hardly wait to eat every **drop** of the soup.
>
> He waited for the water to boil to **drop** the stone into the pot.

A dictionary lists all the different meanings of a word.

Rule Box

You can look at how a word is used in a sentence to help you understand what it means.

- A drop of soup is a small amount of soup.
- Drop the stone into the pot means to let the stone fall.

Practice

Look up each word in the dictionary.
Write two different definitions for each word.

1. trade   4. fill

2. charge   5. carry

3. stone

Fluency
Read with Expression

When you read aloud, use your voice to show feelings.

Practice

Read silently.	▸	Read aloud.	▸	Get comments.	▸	Read aloud again.

"What are you doing?" asked a little girl, who had been watching him from a nearby garden.

"I'm making stone soup," John told her.

"Stone soup!" she cried. "Is it good?"

"You've never had stone soup?" he asked. "Stone soup is delicious!"

The little girl peeked into the pot of water. She saw the stone at the bottom of the pot.

"I have some extra potatoes," she told him. "Would potatoes be good in stone soup?"

"I like stone soup just as it is," John said. "But I think potatoes will make it even better."

The little girl smiled. "Let's put them in!" she said as she dropped the potatoes into the boiling water.

Comprehension

Events in a Plot

The **plot** tells the events that happen in a story. The **events** are the major actions that take place.

Retell

Retell the story to a partner.

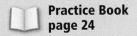 Ask your partner to respond to the Big Question for this reading.

Practice Book
page 24

Practice

Read this list of events and details from *Stone Soup*. **Which ones are major events in the plot? Which ones are details?**

   a. John is hungry. He has a pot but no food.

   b. The farmer's wife thinks John is a nice boy. She wishes she could help him.

   c. John finds a smooth, round stone. The stone gives him an idea.

   d. There were many other stones on the road, but none of them were as smooth or round.

   e. John fills his pot with water and drops the stone in when the water is boiling.

   f. The fire takes a long time to heat the water. John looks for more wood to burn.

Use a Sequence Chart

Events in a story happen in order. That order is called the **sequence**. A Sequence Chart can help you put the events in order, from what happened first to what happened last.

Practice

Create a Sequence Chart for *Stone Soup*.

- Use the three major events you found on page 46.
- Add other events from the list below.
- Then answer the questions at the bottom.

> John shares his soup with the villagers.
>
> The villagers bring small bits of food to add to the soup.
>
> A little girl sees John and offers to add potatoes to the stone soup.

Sequence Chart
1.
2.
3.
4.
5.
6.

1. What event in the story happened before line 1?

2. What event in the story happened after line 6?

3. If this story continued, what do you think would happen next?

47

Grammar & Writing

Future Tense Verbs

In *Stone Soup*, John says to himself, "This soup will be delicious!" He also meets a girl and a boy and asks them, "Will you stay and share this soup with me?" In each of these sentences, John uses the future tense of a verb. **Future tense verbs** name an action that will happen in the future.

Rule Box

To form the future tense of a verb, use the helping verb *will*.

be	⟶	will be	carry	⟶	will carry
stay	⟶	will stay	eat	⟶	will eat

Practice

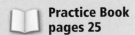
Practice Book pages 25

Copy each verb. Write the future tense form.

1. cook
2. share
3. meet
4. bring
5. ask
6. enjoy

Write a Paragraph

A paragraph contains a topic sentence that states the main idea. Supporting sentences give more information about the main idea. You can use the future tense to describe events that may happen in the future.

Read about how Lino described his uncle's upcoming visit.

I am very excited about next weekend. My uncle is going to come from London for a visit. He said he will take my whole family to Adventure Park for the weekend. We will fly in an airplane. That will be really fun. Then a car will pick us up and take us straight to the park. My sister, my uncle, and I will have a contest to see who can ride the scariest roller coaster. We are going to have a great time.

SPELLING TIP

When trying to spell compound words, look for a smaller word within the larger word:

every + thing = everything

 Practice Book pages 26

Practice

Write a paragraph to describe a fun weekend you would like to have.

- Make sure your paragraph has a topic sentence and several supporting sentences.
- Your paragraph tells about the future, so you will use the future tense.
- Be sure to use the helping verb *will* in your writing.

Writing Checklist

✓ Is your topic sentence clear? Did you give supporting details?

✓ Did you use the future tense in your writing?

✓ Can your partner understand your paragraph?

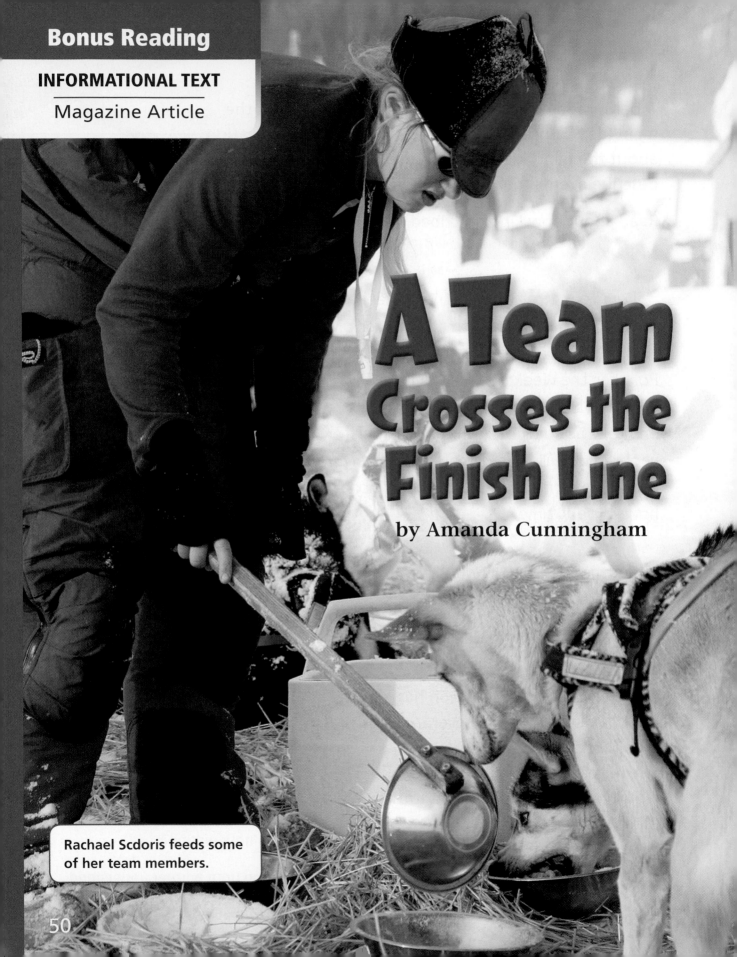

A Team Crosses the Finish Line

by Amanda Cunningham

Rachael Scdoris feeds some of her team members.

Who Is Rachael Scdoris?

Rachael Scdoris is legally blind. She can see very little. What she can see, she cannot see clearly. Rachael was often told that she couldn't do things like run on the track team or race sled dogs. She has done both. In 2006, she became the first legally blind person to finish the world's longest sled dog race.

Rachael has always loved sled dogs. Her father was a sled dog racer, or musher. He raised his own dogs. When Rachael was eight years old, she knew she wanted to be a musher, too.

Rachael learned how to mush by having others ride with her on the sled. Even after she learned, Rachael's father said that someone else had to be on the sled. He wanted to keep Rachael safe. Rachael did not like this. She wanted to race like other mushers. Rachael was not afraid. She kept asking her father to let her drive the sled by herself.

Rachael drove her first sled alone when she was 11 years old. Rachael and her dogs worked as a team. Rachael had to depend on her dogs to follow the trail to the finish line. The dogs had to depend on Rachael to get them to work together. Rachael and her dogs trusted each other. They did well when they raced.

The Big Race

The Iditarod is a famous sled dog race in Alaska. The Iditarod is 1,150 miles long. A legally blind person had never finished it. Rachael wanted to try.

Rachael entered the Iditarod for the first time in 2005. A person on another sled went ahead of Rachael. He told her about obstacles that Rachael could not see. After 700 miles, Rachael had to quit. Some of her dogs were sick. It was hard for them to pull the sled. Rachael knew that she had to support her dogs because her dogs had supported her. She was sad to stop, but her dogs had to come first. They were a team.

An Iditarod racer crosses the finish line with his team of dogs.

Rachael did not give up on her dream of finishing the Iditarod. She kept training herself and her dogs. In 2006, Rachael tried the Iditarod again. She raced for more than 12 days in very cold weather.

Rachael became the first legally blind person to finish the Iditarod. She could not see the finish line, but her dogs led the way. Rachael knew that she and her dogs were able to finish the Iditarod because they had worked together as a team. Rachael and her dogs showed what we can do when we work together.

UNIT 1 Wrap Up

The Big Question

In what ways can people or groups help others?

Written	Oral	Visual/Active
Top Ten List	**Interview**	**Poster**
Write a list of 10 activities kids your age can do to help people where you live. Present the ideas on your list to a partner or group.	Interview someone who spends time helping others. Use the 5W questions for ideas. Share what you learn with a partner or group.	Create a poster about a group that helps people in your community. Tell something about what the group does and how to contact it.
Letter	**Story Share**	**Graphic Organizer**
Write a letter to a group that helps people in your area. Ask how young people can help the group make life better for the people it serves.	Think of a time when someone helped you or your family, or when you helped someone else. Tell your classmates about that time.	Research another group that helps people or animals. Make a chart that shows the information you find.
Flier	**News Watch**	**Event Collage**
Research groups that help people near you. Make a flier for one group that gives important information about it.	Watch or listen to news programs for a few days. Jot down information about events or programs that help people. Present what you learned to the class.	Attend an event where people help others, such as a park cleanup. Make a poster or collage about the event.

✓ Learning Checklist

Word Analysis and Phonics

✓ Identify short vowel sounds.

✓ Practice long vowel sounds with silent e.

✓ Understand that some words can have many meanings.

Comprehension

✓ Preview and predict.

✓ Use a Problem and Solution Chart.

✓ Activate prior knowledge.

✓ Use a KWL Chart.

✓ Identify events in a plot.

✓ Use a Sequence Chart.

Grammar and Writing

✓ Identify singular and plural nouns.

✓ Write a narrative.

✓ Use the past tense.

✓ Write a paragraph with a topic sentence.

✓ Use the future tense.

✓ Write a paragraph with the future tense.

Self-Evaluation Questions

• What did you really learn about helping others?

• How has what you've learned changed your thinking?

• How will you work with others in the future?

55

Heroes and Their Journeys

There are many kinds of heroes. They always have interesting stories.

?

The Big Question

What does it take to be a hero?

READINGS

1

The Three Gifts

2

Brave Androcles

3

The Wizard of Oz

LISTENING AND SPEAKING

You will talk about your favorite heroes and what you think makes them heroes.

WRITING

You will write a poem about your favorite hero.

Quick Write

What does being a hero mean to you? Write down your ideas and share them with a partner.

Bonus Reading

The Elephant Shepherd

What Do You Know about Heroes?

Words to Know

1. Use these words to talk about heroes.

 creative

 strong

 wise

 helpful

 courageous

 athletic

---

2. Who can be a hero?

A hero can be _____ .

 a paramedic

 a firefighter

 a service animal

 me

 a volunteer

3. How can a hero help?

A _____ can help by _____ .

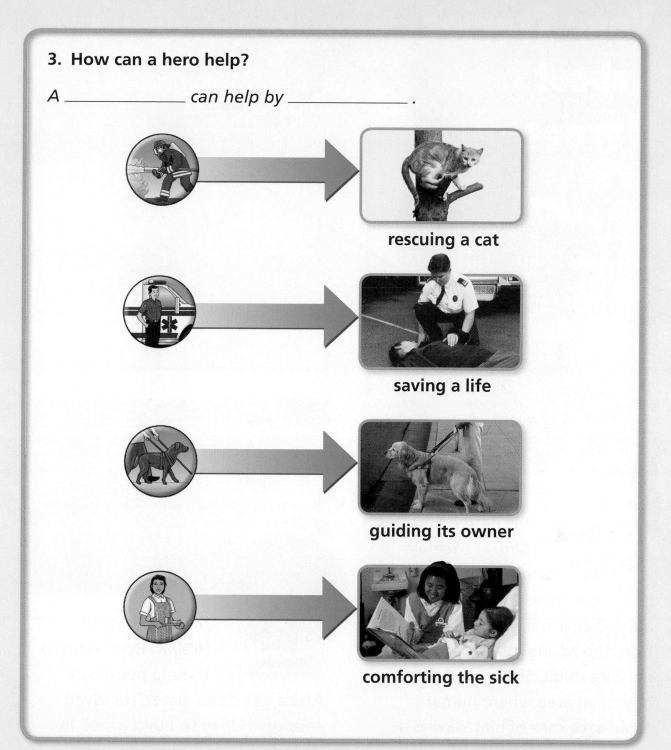

rescuing a cat

saving a life

guiding its owner

comforting the sick

Your Stories about Heroes

Canada

Illinois, U.S.A.

Charlene

My hero is Binti. Binti is a female gorilla who lives in a zoo in Illinois. She rescued a three-year-old boy who fell from the railing into a zoo's gorilla exhibit. She carried the boy to an area where humans could take care of him. Binti is a very caring animal!

Sophie

My hero is Ryan Hreljac. Ryan wanted to help people in Africa get clean water. He saved enough money to build a well in Uganda. He was so happy with the result that he decided to help build more wells. His organization, Ryan's Well, raises money to build wells all over Africa.

Dai

My hero is Jackie Chan. He stars in martial arts movies. We were both born in Hong Kong, an administrative region of China. He started the Jackie Chan Charitable Foundation in Hong Kong and Japan. This organization gives scholarships to needy students. He also has organizations to help the elderly and to give coats to homeless people. Jackie Chan is a great guy!

Panut

My hero is a woman from my country, Indonesia. Butet Manurung wanted to educate children who lived in the Jambi Forest. She volunteered to teach the Anak Dalam people how to read and write. Now Butet lives in the Jambi Forest. Butet's new goal is to teach people from other tribes, too.

What about you?

1 Who is a hero to you? Why?

2 How are these students' stories similar to yours?

3 Do you have a story about a hero? Tell your story!

61

The Three Gifts

Vocabulary

The Three Gifts is a folk tale about how an African leader and his children learn the gift of giving.

Words in Context

1 A job gets done much faster when people **cooperate.**

2 The apple tree **bore** a lot of fruit.

3 Lisa and her friends had a **marvelous** time at the party.

Key Words

- cooperate
- bore
- marvelous
- millet
- virtue
- grateful

④ Have you ever tasted **millet?** It is a grain, like wheat and oats.

⑤ A **virtue** is something that is good about a person. Some people think neatness is a virtue.

⑥ People often show that they are **grateful,** or thankful, when having a feast with family and friends.

Practice

Use each key word in a sentence.

Make Connections

Think of one of your heroes. What do you admire, or like, about him or her? What do you dislike?

Academic Words

assess

evaluate; decide how good or significant something is

error

mistake

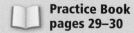

Practice Book pages 29–30

LITERATURE

Folktale

The Big Question

What gifts do heroes bring?

Reading Strategy

Identify Characters and Plot

Stories have a plot, or story line, that is usually a sequence of events. Stories also have characters, which are people or animals.

- Read the title.
- Look at the illustrations.
- Which characters are saying or doing something?
- What do you think is happening in the story?

The Three Gifts

by Shannon Doyne
illustrated by Soud

In Africa, there once was a leader named Jelani. He was a just leader. He cared about his people very much. The people in the village were happy and peaceful.

Jelani had three daughters and four sons. At school, Jelani's children learned about other places in Africa. In some villages, people were hungry. Crops did not grow well. Trees bore no fruit. In other villages, groups of people did not cooperate. They fought fiercely with each other.

Jelani's oldest daughter was named Ada. One night she said, "People in this village have marvelous lives. I want to travel to other places and do what I can to help others."

Jelani looked at her proudly. He said, "Finish school. Then you can help others."

That is just what Ada did.

---

just treating people the same, no matter who they are

fiercely hard

64

When Ada finished school, she went to other villages where she worked hard to help people. Ada's brothers and sisters admired her. She sent drawings of the school she helped to build. Ada wrote that it was a big job, but lots of fun.

One by one, Ada's brothers and sisters finished school. They all asked Jelani if they could go and help people. Jelani's eyes filled with joy each time, and he said, "Yes, you can help people."

In time, only the youngest son remained at home. His name was Kofi. Kofi loved to receive his siblings' letters. One brother helped dig wells for fresh water. Another brother helped farmers plant better crops. A sister helped a village hold an election to choose a better leader.

All of the letters were alike in one way. They all invited Kofi and Jelani to visit their villages.

---

admired   looked up to

siblings   brothers and sisters

election   contest won by the person who gets the most votes

CheckUp Why did Jelani's children want to help people?

65

Kofi and Jelani decided to visit their family. Early one morning, they set out on their horses. They brought with them many of Jelani's advisors.

Late in the first day, they stopped to rest. Some people came out to meet them. They took a great interest in the horses. But their eyes looked sad. "What's wrong?" Kofi asked.

A woman replied, "We have horses, too. But we can't grow the right grains for them. Our horses' health is poor."

"Bring some sacks of millet," Jelani called to his men. "We can feed your horses and leave some sacks for you."

"We are so grateful," the people said. "Someday, we will repay this favor. Just call on us."

---

advisors   people who help others decide what to do

grains   crops such as wheat and oats

favor   kind or helpful act

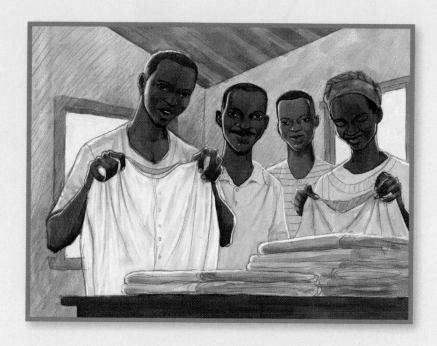

The next day, the group went to the village of Kofi's older brother. His name was Sekou. Sekou hugged Jelani and Kofi tightly. "I have missed you so much!" he said.

Sekou showed Jelani and Kofi the well he had helped to dig. "Another problem is the harsh sun," Sekou said. "Many people do not have the right clothing to protect them. I gave away all of my extra clothes. But so many people still need clothes."

When Jelani and Kofi departed a few days later, they left behind all the extra clothing they had. The villagers told Sekou, "One day, we will find a way to thank them. Please tell this to your father and brother. All they have to do is ask."

---

well   deep hole in the ground where water is found

harsh   strong or painful

departed   left

Check Up   How did Kofi and Jelani help the people in Sekou's village?

The next day, Kofi told his father, "I want to help people, too." Once again, Jelani felt great joy. All of Jelani's children shared the virtue of caring for others.

Just then, they passed several people. They were building a wood house, but they were having a difficult time. "Father," Kofi asked, "many of our men have learned to work with wood. Can we help them?"

Jelani called out, "Stop, everyone!" Jelani's advisors were soon teaching the others how to build a wood house. The people said, "You have helped us with this house. Now we can use these skills to build a whole village. One day, you will call on us, and we will return this favor."

The last stop was Ada's village. But something seemed very wrong. Kofi and Jelani saw there were piles of wood and mud and rocks where houses had once been. Kofi found Ada. "We had a terrible mudslide," Ada said. "Everyone's homes are gone."

---

several many

difficult hard

terrible very bad

Kofi, Jelani, Ada, the advisors, and people from the village started to work. They rebuilt houses. Everyone was very tired and hot. They were also out of supplies. Jelani sent his advisors for help.

Soon, 20 horses appeared. All of the horses had riders. Many of the horses also carried bags of supplies.

"You helped us when we had no food for our horses," one of the riders called. "We came to help you carry supplies."

Many more people appeared. One called out, "You taught us to build houses. Now we can help you."

People from Sekou's village put up a large tent. "You gave us your extra clothes. We stitched them together. You can live in this tent until the new houses are ready."

And together, they rebuilt Ada's village.

---

supplies   things that are needed
stitched   sewed

📖 **Practice Book**
pages 31–32

Reading Strategy

Identify Characters and Plot

- Who are the main characters in the story?
- What are three events in the plot?

Think It Over

1 What do Jelani's children learn in school?

2 What does Kofi receive that makes him want to visit his brothers and sisters?

3 How do the people in the other villages help Ada's village?

Phonics & Fluency

Phonics

Long Vowel Pairs

Long vowel sounds can be spelled in different ways.

Long Vowel Pairs				
Long *a*	**Long *e***	**Long *i***	**Long *o***	**Long *u***
day	meet	lie	oats	cue
grain	seat		doe	fruit

Did you notice that each word has two vowels together?
Which one of the vowels says its name?

Rule Box

When there are two vowels together, the first vowel is usually long, and the second vowel is silent. The vowel pairs below usually have long vowel sounds.

ay, ai	ee, ea	ie	oa, oe	ue, ui

Practice

Work with a partner. Take turns reading the words in the box.

need	pay	three
tried	coast	say
fail	tie	plain
road	due	fruit
clue		

1. Make a chart like the one above.

Practice Book

📖

page 33

2. List the words from this box in the chart.

3. Add two more words for each long vowel sound.

70

Fluency

Look Ahead

Sometimes readers look for hard words before they read. They then try to figure them out.

| Pick one passage. | Find any hard words. | Practice saying those words. | Read the passage aloud. |

1 Jelani's children decide to help people in other villages when they grow up. Later, when one of them needs help, they receive help in return.

2 One by one, Ada's brothers and sisters finished school. They all asked Jelani if they could go and help people. Jelani's eyes filled with joy each time, and he said, "Yes, you can help people."

In time, only the youngest son remained at home. His name was Kofi. Kofi loved to receive his siblings' letters.

3 "Father," Kofi asked, "many of our men have learned to work with wood. Can we help them?"

Jelani called out, "Stop, everyone!" Jelani's advisors were soon teaching the others how to build a wood house. The people said, "You have helped us with this house. Now we can use these skills to build a whole village. One day, you will call on us, and we will return this favor."

Comprehension

Characters and Plot

Every story has **characters**. The characters are the people, or sometimes animals, in the story. Every story also has a **plot**. The plot is the series of events that take place in the story.

Practice

Work with a partner. Make a chart like the one below.

1. Reread the story. Pay attention to the characters and events.

2. List characters and events in the chart. Follow the examples given.

3. Write a short summary of the story.

Learning Strategy

Retell

Retell the story to a partner.

 Ask your partner to respond to the Big Question for this reading.

Practice Book

page 34

72

Character	What Happens	The Result
Jelani	Ada asks him if she can leave.	Jelani tells her to finish school.
Kofi	Gets letters from siblings to visit	Visits siblings with Jelani
Sekou	Gives away clothes	Jelani and Kofi give villagers extra clothing.

Use a Cause and Effect Chart

When one thing happens, it causes other things to happen. A Cause and Effect Chart helps you see how events in a plot are related.

Practice

Work with a partner. Copy this Cause and Effect Chart.

1. Add one more effect to the chart.

2. List two more causes.

3. Show what effects those events caused.

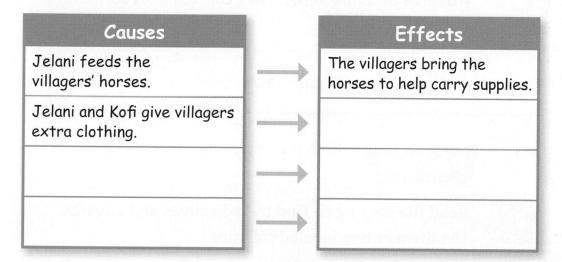

Causes	Effects
Jelani feeds the villagers' horses.	The villagers bring the horses to help carry supplies.
Jelani and Kofi give villagers extra clothing.	

Extension

Some people say it is better to give than to receive. Think about causes and effects in terms of something you have done for someone else. What was the effect of what you did? Why did you decide to do what you did? Present your experience to the class using a visual aid.

Grammar & Writing

Adjectives and Adverbs

Adjectives and adverbs tell more about other words. **Adjectives** tell more about nouns. They can tell what someone or something is like.

> In some villages, the people were **hungry**.

Adverbs describe verbs. They can tell how something happens or is done.

> Jelani looked at her **proudly**.

Practice

Read the sentences. Find the adjectives and adverbs. List them in two labeled columns.

1. Jelani was a fair man.

2. The strong people fought fiercely.

3. The tired villagers thanked Kofi and Jelani.

4. The villagers gladly helped Ada at the end.

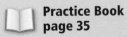
Practice Book page 35

74

Write about Causes and Effects

When you write about causes and effects, it is important to describe both the cause and the effect. Read how Zaheda described one cause and effect in *The Three Gifts*.

> Kofi and his family wanted to help people who were not as lucky as they were. On their way to visit Ada, Kofi and Jelani met some villagers who were having a hard time building a house. Kofi and Jelani stopped to help. They taught the people in the village how to build houses. Later, when Ada's village was destroyed in a mudslide, the villagers remembered. They helped Ada rebuild her village.

SPELLING TIP

When the letters *c* and *h* or *s* and *h* are together in a word, they make one sound.

Practice Book page 36

Practice

Write your own cause and effect paragraph.

1. Think about a situation.

2. Write what you think caused the situation.

3. Write one good or bad effect of that cause.

4. Write a concluding sentence that summarizes the cause and effect.

Writing Checklist

✓ Did you describe the situation?

✓ Did you identify one cause of the situation?

✓ Did you describe one effect from that cause?

✓ Can a partner understand your paragraph?

Brave Androcles

Vocabulary

Brave Androcles is a poem about a boy and a lion who become heroes to each other.

Words in Context

Key Words

chased

arena

swollen

wander

criminal

1 The lion **chased** the warthog.

2 This **arena** was built almost 2,000 years ago in Rome.

3 The bee sting made his hand **swollen.**

4 It is fun to **wander** down by a stream on a nice summer's day.

5 The police officer arrested the **criminal.**

Practice

Use each key word in a sentence.

Make Connections

The place where the early Romans went to watch sports and games was called an arena. What are the names of other places where sports and games are played?

Academic Words

motive
underlying reason

principle
basic truth; rule

Practice Book
pages 37–38

LITERATURE

Poetry

The Big Question

What is meant by "one good deed deserves another"?

Reading Strategy

Make Connections

- As you read the poem, think of moments in your own life when you have felt like Androcles.

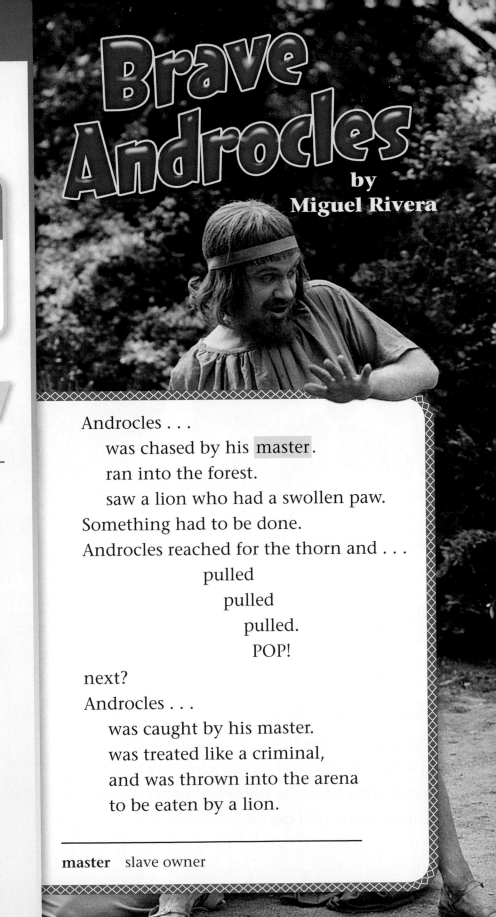

Brave Androcles

by
Miguel Rivera

Androcles . . .
   was chased by his master.
   ran into the forest.
   saw a lion who had a swollen paw.
Something had to be done.
Androcles reached for the thorn and . . .
        pulled
          pulled
            pulled.
         POP!

next?
Androcles . . .
   was caught by his master.
   was treated like a criminal,
   and was thrown into the arena
   to be eaten by a lion.

---

master   slave owner

Not just any ordinary lion, his friend.
The lion was as sweet as sugar.
He was as quiet as a mouse.
All he did was wander around the arena.
He did not . . .
　　　　　bite.
　　　　　eat.
　　　　　growl.
next?
Master was . . .
　　　　　shocked.
　　　　　amazed
　　　　　confused.
And Androcles was a hero.
Never bothered again,
　　　　　　　　WHEW!

---

ordinary　average

amazed　surprised

confused　unable to think clearly

**Practice Book
pages 39–40**

Reading Strategy

Make Connections

- When have you done something even though you were scared to do it?

- In what ways are you like Androcles?

Think It Over

1 Who is Androcles?

2 What problem does the lion have?

3 Why does the lion help Androcles?

4 How are Androcles and the lion alike?

Phonics & Fluency

Phonics

Vowel Pair: *ea*

Each word in the chart has the vowel pair *ea*.

Vowel Pair *ea*			
Long e		**Short e**	
eat	plead	head	sweat
sea	speak	bread	death
teach		spread	

The vowel pair *ea* can stand for two sounds.

Rule Box

The vowel pair *ea* can have the long e sound, as in **eat,** or the short e sound, as in **head**. If you come across a word you do not know, try reading it both ways!

Practice

Read the sentences in the box with a partner.

1. List the words in which *ea* has the long e sound.

2. List the words in which *ea* has the short e sound.

3. Add two more words to each list.

- I can read about heroes.
- Some heroes reach out to others.
- Some heroes work hard to get ahead.
- Some heroes fight in deadly battles.

Practice Book

page 41

80

Fluency

Read with Expression

When you read aloud, use your voice to show feelings.

Practice

Read silently.		Read aloud.		Get comments.		Read aloud again.

1 Androcles . . .
        was chased by his master.
        ran into the forest.
        saw a lion who had a swollen paw.
Something had to be done.
Androcles reached for the thorn and . . .
               pulled
                  pulled
                     pulled.
                       POP!

Comprehension

Make Connections

One way to understand a text is to make connections between what happens in the text and your life.

Learning Strategy

Retell

Retell the poem to a partner.

 Ask your partner to respond to the Big Question for this reading.

Practice

- Read the first column. It tells about situations in the story.
- Answer the questions in the second column to tell about similar situations in your life.

Situations in the Story	Situations in Your Life
1. Androcles was chased by his master.	1. When have you been scared?
2. The lion has a problem.	2. What kinds of problems have you had?
3. Androcles and the lion become friends.	3. What happened afterward?
4. Androcles gets helps from the lion to solve his problem.	4. Who helped you with your problem?

Practice Book
page 42

Use a Story Map

You can use a Story Map to help you better understand
a story or poem.

Practice

Copy this Story Map. Complete it to show the main characters,
the setting, and what happens in *Brave Androcles*.

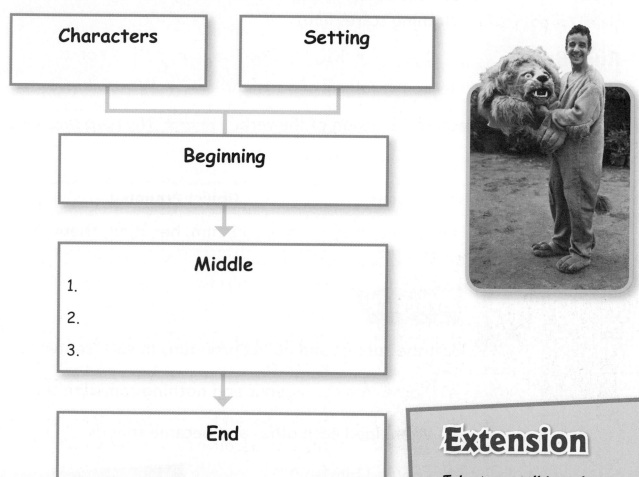

Characters	Setting

Beginning

Middle

1.

2.

3.

End

Extension

Take turns talking about
good deeds you have
done with a partner.
Then describe something
that happened as a
result of your good deed.

Grammar & Writing

Pronouns

Pronouns take the place of nouns. In these sentences, the pronouns are in red.

Androcles is a young boy. **He** is very courageous. Nothing scares **him**.

Rule Box

Subject pronouns refer to the subject of a sentence. ⟶ **We** are *brave*.

Object pronouns receive the action of the verb. ⟶ *The hero saved* **us**.

Subject Pronouns	Object Pronouns
I, you, he, she, it, we, they	me, you, him, her, it, us, them

Practice

List the subject and object pronouns in each sentence.

1. Heroes are courageous and nothing can scare them.

2. We helped each other and became friends.

3. I helped him.

4. Padma said she enjoyed the poem.

5. It is a poem about a young hero!

Practice Book page 43

Write a Poem

Poems use patterns and sounds to express ideas and emotions. Some poems have lines that rhyme, and some poems don't. Groups of lines, called **verses**, give the poem a nice rhythm.

Read Michael's poem:

> He walks through flames.
> He climbs high-rises.
> He puts out fires
> Without surprises!
>
> He can help rescue
> Your cat from a tree,
> Or he can show the firehouse
> To you and to me!

SPELLING TIP

When the letter *c* is followed by *a*, *o*, or *u*, as in *cat*, *cone*, or *cub*, it stands for the sound /k/.

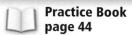 **Practice Book page 44**

Practice

1. Who is the hero of this poem?

2. How many verses does the poem have?

3. Write a poem about your favorite hero. Remember to use a capital letter to start each verse.

Writing Checklist

✔ Did you use pronouns in your poem? Underline them.

✔ Did all your verses start with a capital letter?

✔ Can a partner understand your poem?

The Wizard of Oz

Vocabulary

In this retelling of *The Wizard of Oz*, Dorothy falls asleep at home on the farm and wakes up in a strange place.

Words in Context

Key Words

blister
contained
broad
midst
merry
startle

1 The paint was so old that it started to **blister.**

2 Jake took out a book about his favorite artist. It **contained** many pretty illustrations of the artist's work.

3 Many people can drive cars on this **broad** avenue at the same time.

86

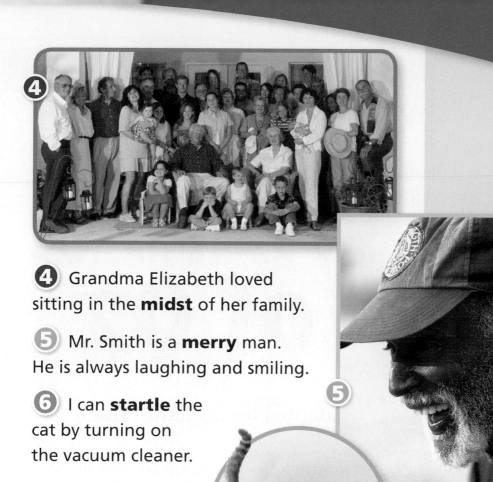

4 Grandma Elizabeth loved sitting in the **midst** of her family.

5 Mr. Smith is a **merry** man. He is always laughing and smiling.

6 I can **startle** the cat by turning on the vacuum cleaner.

Practice

Use each key word in a sentence.

Make Connections

Is being in a strange situation scary, exciting, or both? Describe a time you were in a strange situation.

Academic Words

distinct

separate; different from others

---

interact

act upon or with another

Practice Book pages 45–46

The **Big** Question

Can ordinary people become heroes? How?

Reading Strategy

Identify Problems and Solutions

You may know the story of *The Wizard of Oz*. Look through this reading.

- What problem do you think Dorothy has?
- What solutions might she find?

The Wizard of Oz

adapted by Leonard Pringle

Dorothy's life was good, but boring. She lived on a farm in Kansas with her Uncle Henry and Aunt Em. "There's nothing to do here," she said to herself many times a day. She stared and stared at the broad, gray fields. She waited for something to happen.

The sun came up every day. It often got hot enough to blister the paint on the house's walls. Then the sun set. Dorothy didn't notice. Each day was like the other.

Dorothy loved her aunt and uncle. They were kind to her. Uncle Henry and Aunt Em just did not know how to help a bored and lonely young girl.

---

notice pay attention to

It was a good thing that Dorothy had Toto, her little, black dog. Toto had merry eyes and funny, little teeth. It always looked like he was smiling. Dorothy would laugh at her silly, little dog. She would say, "Oh, Toto, you are my only friend in the world."

During one boring day, the wind started to howl. Uncle Henry came running from the field. He yelled, "There's a tornado coming! Em! Dorothy! Let's get in the cellar!"

Uncle Henry's voice was loud enough to startle Toto. He jumped out of Dorothy's arms and hid under the bed. She ran after him.

"Hurry, Dorothy!" Aunt Em called from the cellar stairs. Her voice sounded quiet in the midst of the windy storm.

---

tornado   powerful wind storm with funnel-shaped clouds

cellar   basement

Dorothy thought life on the farm in Kansas was boring.

Check Up   Why is Dorothy bored?

89

Dorothy crawled under the bed and grabbed Toto. As she was standing up, the house seemed to shake. She fell down. Something seemed to keep her from standing up. "Oh!" Dorothy cried. "Aunt Em!"

Only the howling wind answered. Under the house, the strong storm winds met with a crash. Dorothy knew that she, Toto, and the house were in the center of the tornado. As the winds grew stronger, they lifted up the house like a balloon.

A second later, the house started to spin around. Once, twice, three times, it went around in a circle!

Dorothy stayed on the floor. The house was carried far away from Kansas. Soon, Dorothy felt like she was being rocked to sleep. In time, she did fall asleep.

---

center middle

A tornado lifted Dorothy's house up, up, and away!

Dorothy was startled when she woke up. The house had landed gently on the ground. Bright sunshine poured through the windows' unbroken panes.

A beautiful new world appeared. There were huge flowers, tall trees, and a small, sparkling brook.

Dorothy meets the Munchkins.

It was nothing like the farm in Kansas.

A group of people walked toward Dorothy. They were all very small. Their clothes contained every color of the rainbow. Dorothy thought they were children. Then she saw that some of the people had long beards. Some of the people had white hair and wrinkled faces.

"Welcome to Oz, brave witch," a woman said. "We are so grateful to you for killing the Wicked Witch of the East. Now the Munchkins are free!"

---

gently   softly

panes   pieces of glass

brook   small stream

CheckUp How did the Munchkins react to Dorothy?

"You are very kind," Dorothy said, "but I'm afraid you are mistaken. I didn't kill anyone."

The woman smiled and said, "Well, your house killed someone. Come and look."

Dorothy looked down. Sure enough, two feet stuck out from under the house. The feet wore red shoes.

"Oh, dear," Dorothy cried. "The house must have fallen on her. What can we do to help her?"

"Nothing," the woman replied. "I'm afraid it is too late."

A new person appeared. She wore a pretty gown, and she was much taller than the Munchkins.

"Hello, Dorothy. I am Glinda, the Witch of the North," the new woman said. "I came to tell you that those shoes now belong to you."

Dorothy looked down at the red shoes. Then she looked back at the Witch of the North. "Really?" Dorothy said.

---

mistaken   wrong

gown   long dress

Dorothy gets red shoes from the Witch of the North.

Just then, Glinda waved her long, silver wand in a circle around the shoes. There was a puff of smoke. Dorothy blinked. Suddenly, she was wearing the red shoes.

"Thank you," Dorothy said. "I have to go home now. Can you tell me how to get back to Kansas? I am sure I am late for supper."

"You will have to find that out for yourself," Glinda said.

This was the beginning of Dorothy's adventures in Oz.

---

blinked   opened and closed quickly

Dorothy meets the Wicked Witch of the West, the Scarecrow, the Tin Man, and the Cowardly Lion in Oz.

Practice Book pages 47–48

Reading Strategy

Identify Problems and Solutions

Before you read the story, you thought about the problems that Dorothy might face.

- What problems are solved in the story?
- What new problems does Dorothy find?

Think It Over

1 What does Dorothy think of her life in Kansas?

2 How does Toto make Dorothy's life happier?

3 Where does the tornado take Dorothy?

4 What adventures do you think Dorothy will have?

Word Analysis & Fluency

Word Analysis

Word Origins

Like many words in English, the word **tornado** comes from another language. **Tornado** is a form of the Spanish word **tronada**, which means thunderstorm. What do you know about tornadoes?

Practice

Read the clues below. Match each clue with a word from the box.

mistaken
cellar
pane
gown
notice

1. This word is taken from the Latin word **cella**, which means "small room" or "storeroom."

2. This word can be traced back to the Latin word **noscere**, which means "to get to know."

3. This word for "a piece of glass" is from the French word **pan**, meaning "piece."

4. This word is a form of the Norse word **mistaka**, which means "to take in error."

5. This word for "long dress" is from the French word **goune**, which means "long coat."

Fluency

Read for Speed and Accuracy

You should read quickly. But never read so quickly that you lose your understanding.

Practice

| Read for one minute. | Count the words you read. | Study any hard words. | Read and count again. |

Dorothy's life was good, but boring. She lived on a farm in   12
Kansas with her Uncle Henry and Aunt Em.   20

"There's nothing to do here," she said to herself many   30
times a day. She stared and stared at the broad, gray fields. She 43
waited for something to happen.   48

The sun came up every day. It often got hot enough to   60
blister the paint on the house's walls. Then the sun set. Dorothy 72
didn't notice. Each day was like the other.   80

Dorothy loved her aunt and uncle. They were always kind   90
to her. Uncle Henry and Aunt Em just did not know how to   103
help a bored and lonely young girl.   110

It was a good thing that Dorothy had Toto, her little, black   122
dog. Toto had merry eyes and funny, little teeth. It always looked 134
like he was smiling. Dorothy would laugh at her silly, little dog. 146
She would say, "Oh, Toto, you are my only friend in the world."   159

Comprehension

Characters and Conflicts

A **conflict** is a disagreement. A story can have more than one conflict. A conflict can be within the character, between different characters, or between a character and an event.

Learning Strategy

Outline

Make an outline of the main characters and events in the story.

Share your outline with a partner.

 Ask your partner to respond to the Big Question for this reading.

Practice

Tell whether the conflict is within one character, between characters, or between a character and an event. Sometimes there is more than one correct answer.

1. Dorothy had a good life on the farm, but she was bored.

2. Uncle Henry and Aunt Em did not know how to help Dorothy.

3. Aunt Em tried to get Dorothy to go to the cellar.

4. Dorothy tried to keep Toto safe from the tornado.

5. Dorothy wants to explore Oz, but she also wants to go home.

 Practice Book page 50

Use an Idea Web

An Idea Web can help you see how different ideas in a story are connected.

Practice

Copy this Idea Web. Complete it to show what you know about Dorothy's conflicts.

- Share your work with a partner.
- Discuss how you think Dorothy will solve the conflicts she faces.

Dorothy's conflicts with herself

Dorothy's conflicts in Kansas

Dorothy

Dorothy's conflicts with other characters

Dorothy's conflicts in Oz

Extension

Describe a strange situation or place you found yourself in. Draw a picture of your experience. Then share what you drew with the class.

Grammar & Writing

Possessive Nouns

When you use **possessive nouns**, you are saying something belongs to a person. If you want to talk about shoes that belong to your sister, you might say, "my sister's shoes."

Rule Box

To make a singular noun possessive, add an apostrophe (') and **s**. Example: **girl's** dog

To make a plural noun possessive, you add an apostrophe (') after the **s**. Example: the **boys'** lunchboxes.

To make a plural noun that does not end in *s* possessive, add an apostrophe and *s*. Example: **children's** toys.

Practice

Tell whether the underlined noun is singular or plural. Rewrite the phrase, using the possessive form.

1. the dog belonging to <u>Amy</u>

2. the hat belonging to <u>Mrs. Smith</u>

3. the roofs belonging to the <u>houses</u>

4. the meeting the <u>women</u> went to

Practice Book page 51

Write a Descriptive Paragraph

Look. Sniff. Feel. Use your senses to help you write. What does a thing look like? Smell or taste like? What does it feel like when you touch it? What sounds do you hear if you tap it?

Notice the words Sophia used to describe a room in her home.

The best thing in my dad's house is the giant playroom. My brother and I use our imaginations and become whatever we want. I can be a fearless superhero. I can swing from tall buildings and onto dark rooftops, where I step into slick, wet puddles.

My brother likes to paint bright, colorful paintings. He painted a slick, silver race car with a black roof. He says it's his dream car. I said that I don't need a car. I'll just use my speedy, sturdy wings to fly as fast as a rocket ship.

What's that? I can smell something sweet. Time to become me again and have some of the hot, fresh cookies Dad baked. Mmm!

SPELLING TIP

An apostrophe (') takes the place of letters left out in words like **don't**.

 Practice Book page 52

Practice

Write about a room in your home.

- Choose a room.
- Explore it with all your senses.
- List things you see, feel, smell, and hear. Then write your description.

Writing Checklist

✓ Did you describe what you saw, smelled, touched, or tasted?

✓ Can a partner see what you are describing?

99

The Elephant Shepherd

retold by Abdoul Tafari
illustrated by Gary Torrisi

Ousmane was finally old enough to watch the cattle by himself. He loved spending his days on top of the hill looking over the savanna. He knew he had an important job to do. Ousmane's father, Amadou, told him that the family needed the cattle to survive.

One hot, sunny day, Ousmane was standing on the hill watching the cattle. The cattle were grazing calmly. Then Ousmane heard loud stomping noises. He thought a giant was coming. The cattle looked up.

Ousmane saw what was making the noise. It was a herd of elephants. Ousmane was so excited. His father had told him about elephants, but he had never seen one. Ousmane liked watching the baby elephant with its mother the best.

"Ousmane!"

Suddenly, Ousmane saw his father, Amadou, running toward the elephants. "Shoo!" "Shoo!" Amadou yelled at the elephants. The elephants started to move away. The baby elephant looked scared and walked close to its mother.

"Why did you scare the elephants away?" asked Ousmane.

"I like the elephants, too. But we need the grass for our cattle," Amadou replied. "If the elephants stomp on the grass, the cattle will have nothing to eat."

Ousmane was sad. That night at supper, Ousmane told Amadou that he hoped the mother and baby elephant would come back to visit when there was more grass for the cattle.

Ousmane dreamed about the mother and baby elephant that night.

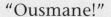

Early the next day, Ousmane and Amadou set out to find good grass for their cattle. They came across an elephant on the ground. They were shocked to see that the elephant's tusks had been sawed off.

"Poachers," said Amadou. "They take the tusks and sell them for money. It is against the law, but some people don't care."

"Why would someone want to hurt the elephants?" Ousmane asked sadly.

Ousmane and Amadou walked on and came upon the rest of the elephant herd. They watched the elephants for a little while and then went back to tend their cattle.

Ousmane thought about the elephants all day. He wished he could stop the poachers.

Ousmane and Amadou took their cattle to a pasture near the elephants the next day. The elephants were eating leaves off some trees. Ousmane and Amadou stopped to watch.

"They are such beautiful, strong creatures," Amadou said. "Look how nicely the baby elephant and the adults are getting along."

"Do you think they are related?" Ousmane asked.

"Probably," replied Amadou. "Elephants have families like we do."

When he returned to school the following week, Ousmane decided to ask his teacher if his classmates could do something to protect the elephants. After school the next day, Ousmane and his classmates started to tell the other villagers why it was important to protect the elephants from poachers.

The Big Question

What does it take to be a hero?

Written	Oral	Visual/Active
Definition	**Discussion**	**Magazine Cover**
Write your own dictionary definition for the word *hero*. List five people who would fit your definition.	Have a discussion asking: What is the most important quality a hero needs? Give examples to support your choice.	Create a magazine cover that shows one of your heroes and words that describe him or her. Give the magazine a special title.
Story	**Reality Show**	**Hero Cards**
Write a story about a character who becomes a hero. Use the 5 W Questions to describe your hero. Be sure the plot shows how your character becomes a hero.	Work with a group. Have each student describe a hero from real life or from stories. Ask questions, and vote for the most heroic character.	Create a set of cards about heroes. One set of cards should show pictures of heroes. The set of matching cards should describe what the heroes did.
Survey	**News Report**	**Awards Ceremony**
Write a 10-question survey about heroes. Ask your classmates to complete the survey as it relates to their favorite heroes. Report your results to the class.	Create a news story titled *Three More Gifts* in which character A helps character B, who helps character C, and so on. Present your story as a news report.	Design awards for heroes. Create a storyboard for each nominee that tells about the event that made him or her a hero.

✔ Learning Checklist

Word Analysis and Phonics

✓ Pronounce long vowel pairs correctly.

✓ Pronounce the vowel pair *ea* correctly.

✓ Use word origins to determine the meanings of unknown words.

Comprehension

✓ Identify characters and plot.

✓ Use a Cause and Effect Chart.

✓ Make connections between text and self.

✓ Use a Story Map.

✓ Identify characters and conflicts.

✓ Use an Idea Web.

Grammar and Writing

✓ Identify adjectives and adverbs.

✓ Use pronouns correctly.

✓ Use apostrophes to make singular and plural possessives.

✓ Describe causes and effects.

✓ Write a poem.

✓ Write a descriptive paragraph.

Self-Evaluation Questions

• How is a hero similar to or different from other people?

• How does what you've learned connect to other learning?

• How could you learn more about what makes a person a hero?

UNIT 3
Building a New Country

New countries have been created throughout history. When new countries are created, many challenges and opportunities are created, too.

READINGS

1

Writing a Great Speech

2

One Hot Summer in Philadelphia

3

One Out of Many

The Big Question

How do people create new countries?

LISTENING AND SPEAKING

You will talk about how people celebrate the creation of a new country.

WRITING

You will write a speech that persuades someone to agree with you or to take action.

Bonus Reading

The Real Soldier

Quick Write

What do you know about the early history of the United States or your home country? Write down five facts.

What Do You Know about Building a New Country?

Words to Know

1. Use these words to talk about a new country.

 laws

 currency

 flag

 government

 citizens

 language

---

2. Where do people come from?

People come from _____ .

 India

 Mexico

 China

 Nigeria

 Ireland

 Colombia

3. What does a new country need?

A new country needs _____ to _____ .

control traffic

trade

make laws

vote

4. Use these words to talk about country symbols.

bird

national anthem

flower

landmarks

Your Stories about Building a New Country

Pennsylvania, U.S.A.

Mexico

Trinidad & Tobago

Diego

I live in Mexico City, Mexico. I love to walk around the plazas on El Grito, which is September 16. El Grito is the celebration of Mexico's independence from Spain. People decorate every plaza in Mexico City with beautiful lights. They sell flags, sombreros, and food in the streets.

Trinidad

I live in Trinidad. My parents named me Trinidad because I was born on August 31. That's the day that my country celebrates its independence from the United Kingdom. There are many parades and street festivals on Independence Day. It feels as if the whole country is celebrating my birthday!

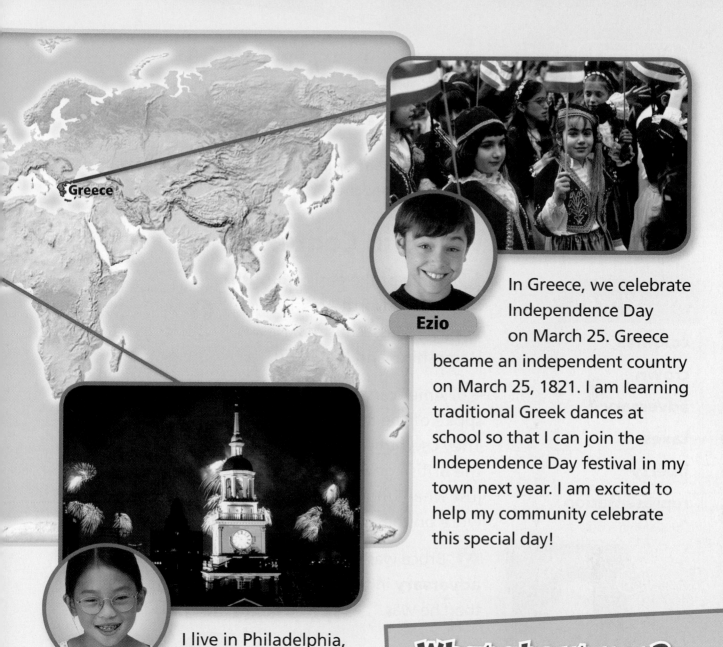

Greece

Ezio

In Greece, we celebrate Independence Day on March 25. Greece became an independent country on March 25, 1821. I am learning traditional Greek dances at school so that I can join the Independence Day festival in my town next year. I am excited to help my community celebrate this special day!

Andie

I live in Philadelphia, Pennsylvania. My city is sometimes called the birthplace of the United States because the U.S. Declaration of Independence was signed here in 1776. Each year on July 4, we have parades and fireworks to celebrate this special day.

What about you?

1 Does your home country celebrate its independence? How do you celebrate?

2 How are these students' stories similar to yours?

3 Do you have a story to tell about your country's independence day? Tell your story!

111

Writing a Great Speech

Vocabulary

Writing a Great Speech is about great speakers and great speeches.

Words in Context

Key Words

- colonies
- crown
- adversary
- taxes
- liberty
- representation

1 Some of the earliest British **colonies** in North America were Virginia, Massachusetts, New Hampshire, and Maryland.

2 American colonists often spoke of the British **crown**. They used this word to mean the British government — not just what kings and queens wore on their heads!

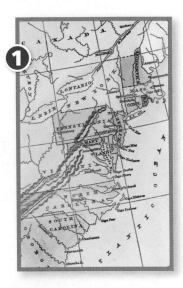

3 Bruce was not worried, even though his **adversary** in the boxing ring was much taller than he was.

4 April 15 is the day Americans must pay their income **taxes** to the U.S. government and their state governments.

5 This statue is a symbol of **liberty**, or freedom, all over the world.

6 In the United States, the voters elect people to give them **representation** in the government.

Practice

Use each key word in a sentence.

Make Connections

People pay taxes to provide money for the government. What are some kinds of taxes that people pay? What does the government do with the money?

Academic Words

contract
legal agreement between two or more people

compensate
pay or reward

Practice Book
pages 55–56

113

The Big Question

Why do people make speeches when new countries are being formed?

Reading Strategy

Compare and Contrast

When you compare, you look for ways in which things are similar. When you contrast, you look for ways in which things are different.

- How are the themes of the speeches similar or different?

- What do the two speeches want their audiences to do?

Writing a Great Speech

by Dan Ahearn

Dr. Martin Luther King, Jr.'s *I Have a Dream* speech was one of the most famous speeches in U.S. history. The theme of King's speech spoke for itself.

First, pick a theme you care about. Be specific. The theme "freedom" is too general. "What freedom means to me" is more specific. Then, think about why you want to give the speech. Do you want people to take action? Do you want people to agree with you? Look for true stories about your theme. These stories will show how your ideas work in real life.

Finally, learn about your audience. What do they already know? What would you like them to learn?

---

theme main idea

specific detailed and exact

audience people listening or watching

Dr. Martin Luther King, Jr. gave one of the most famous speeches in U.S. history.

A speech should have a beginning, a middle, and an end. Make sure each part helps the audience follow your ideas.

The beginning is important. A good beginning gives the speech's theme. The beginning of the speech should also fit the theme. A joke at the start of a speech may not go with a serious theme. A good beginning makes people interested in what you have to say. It will stay in a listener's mind.

The middle of the speech explains your theme. It gives reasons and facts. It should have a true story or a real-life example of your theme.

The ending tells your theme again in a new way. In a few words, connect the theme to your facts. Keep your purpose in mind. End your speech by asking the audience to take action or agree with your ideas.

---

example something that helps explain or support a general idea

purpose goal or result

A good speech keeps your audience interested.

CheckUp What is one difference between a good speech and a bad speech?

Speeches

Boston, Massachusetts, July 1776

INDEPENDENCE NOW . . . OR NEVER!

by Abigail Smith

The colonies must be free of the British crown. Why? The taxes we pay to King George are not fair. He taxes everything, even the news! We do not get anything for what we pay! The king takes away our liberty. We have no representation in England. The king will not even let us pick our own leaders in America. He sends troops to make us do as we are told. You and your family must let these armed men live in your house. Under this king, even your life is not yours. King George is making war against us. British soldiers killed unarmed people in Boston. They might kill you next time. Take action! We do not need a king! We want independence now!

---

troops   soldiers

unarmed   without weapons

independence   freedom of action and choice

Patrick Henry said, "Give me liberty or give me death" in his famous speech.

WE ARE PART OF THE EMPIRE
by Nathan Powell

We need to stay with England. King George is our only chance. The king is not your adversary. We need him. We are British. The taxes we pay are fair. They pay for our defense. Yes, there have been mistakes. But King George took care of these problems. We no longer pay a tax on our papers. We need British troops to protect us. They protect us from people like the Sons of Liberty. The Sons of Liberty were wrong to throw tea into the sea. If things quiet down, we will be left alone. With King George, our lives are safe. Without him, our lives will be very dangerous. Do not do something you will be sorry for. Believe in King George. He believes in us.

---

defense   protection from invaders

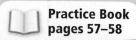

**Practice Book
pages 57–58**

Reading Strategy

Compare and Contrast

- In what ways are the two speeches similar?

- How are the two speeches different?

Think It Over

1 What is the purpose of a good speech?

2 What was the purpose of Abigail Smith's speech?

3 What is the theme of Nathan Powell's speech?

4 What do you need to know in order to write a good speech?

Great American Speakers and Speeches

Abraham Lincoln ▶

Abraham Lincoln gave his *Gettysburg Address* on November 19, 1863. It remains one of the greatest speeches in American history.

César Chávez ▶

César Chávez was a Mexican American labor leader and civil rights activist. His speeches inspired thousands to work for the fair treatment of migrant workers.

▲ Frederick Douglass

Frederick Douglass was a prominent African American author and speaker. His speech, *What to the Slave is the 4th of July?* inspired many people to question their beliefs about equality.

▲ Maya Angelou

Poet Maya Angelou moved many people when she read her poem *On the Pulse of the Morning* during President Bill Clinton's inauguration in 1993.

Sojourner Truth

A former slave, Sojourner Truth became a civil rights activist. Her most famous speech, *Ain't I a Woman?*, was delivered in 1851 at a women's rights convention in Akron, OH.

John F. Kennedy ▶

In his inaugural speech in 1961, President John F. Kennedy inspired Americans to become active citizens. He said, "Ask not what your country can do for you; ask what you can do for your country."

Eleanor Roosevelt

Eleanor Roosevelt was a delegate to the United Nations General Assembly. She chaired the committee that wrote and approved the Universal Declaration of Human Rights.

Barack Obama

Barack Obama gave an important speech at the 2004 Democratic National Convention. The speech made him one of the most popular politicians in the nation.

Activity to Do!

On these pages, you learned about great speakers in American history.

- Choose a speaker.
- Research the speaker.
- Create two pages, using pictures and words, to tell about that speaker.

Phonics & Fluency

Phonics

R-controlled: *ar, or, ore*

Read each pair of words. Notice how the
letter *r* changes the vowel sound.

am	ton	toe
arm	torn	tore

Here are more words with an *r* after a vowel. Read them aloud.

far	or
hard	for
dark	more

Rule Box

The letters *ar* usually have the vowel sound in *arm*.
The letters *or* and *ore* usually have the vowel sound in *torn*.

Practice

Work with a partner. Take turns.

- Read each pair of words.
- Tell whether the words have the same vowel sound.

1. arm, park
2. more, form
3. car, rack
4. care, George
5. sure, soar
6. bore, floor

Fluency

Read for Speed and Accuracy

You should read quickly. But never read so quickly that you lose your understanding.

Practice

| Read for one minute. | Count the words you read. | Study any hard words. | Read and count again. |

We need to stay with England. King George is our only	11
chance. The king is not your adversary. We need him.	21
We are British. The taxes we pay are fair. They pay for our	34
defense. Yes, there have been mistakes. But King George	43
took care of these problems. We no longer pay a tax on our	56
papers. We need British troops to protect us. They protect	66
us from people like the Sons of Liberty. The Sons of Liberty	78
were wrong to throw tea into the sea. If things quiet down,	90
we will be left alone. With King George, our lives are safe.	102
Without him, our lives will be very dangerous. Do not do	113
something you will be sorry for. Believe in King George. He	124
believes in us.	127

Comprehension

Compare and Contrast

One way to understand the ideas you read about is to compare and contrast them. When you **compare**, you tell how two or more things are similar. When you **contrast**, you tell how two or more things are different.

Learning Strategy

Outline

Make an outline of one of the speeches. Show your outline to a partner.

 Ask your partner to respond to the Big Question for this reading.

Practice

Compare and contrast the items described in each pair of words.

1. car and bus

2. apple and orange

3. soccer and football

4. dog and horse

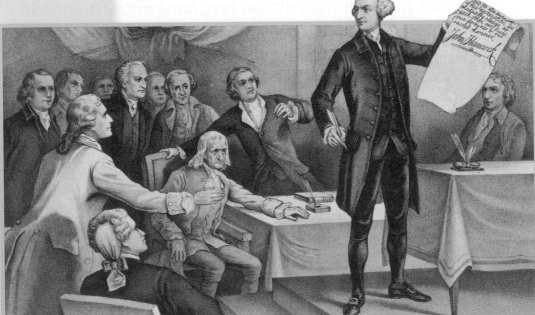

Use a Venn Diagram

You can use a Venn Diagram to compare and contrast events or characters. Circle A represents one item. Circle B represents another. The part that overlaps represents things that are true for both.

Practice

Create a Venn Diagram to compare the speeches.

- Reread the speeches.
- Show how the speeches are similar and different.

A
Abigail Smith

B
Nathan Powell

Extension

Think about a speech you have heard. Answer the 5 W Questions about the speech. Present your answers to the class using part of the speech or a visual aid.

Grammar & Writing

Subject-Verb Agreement

Singular subjects need singular verbs. Plural subjects need plural verbs.

Singular	A good speech **gives** the theme of the speech.
Plural	Good speeches **keep** people interested.

Rules	Examples
When the subject is a singular noun or *he, she,* or *it,* add -s to the verb.	The student **makes** a speech. She **makes** a speech.
When the subject is a plural noun or *I, we, you,* or *they,* do not add -s to the verb.	Her classmates **listen.** They **listen.**

Practice

Write each sentence. Use the correct form of the verb.

1. I _____ my speech carefully. (prepare)

2. You _____ me with the ending. (help)

3. A speech's ending _____ the theme again in a different way. (tell)

4. It _____ the theme once again. (restate)

5. A good speech _____ the audience to action. (move)

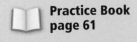
Practice Book page 61

124

Write a Persuasive Speech

When you write a persuasive speech, you want the audience to agree with you or to do something. Read Jose's speech. Think about the ways Jose's speech persuades.

Freedom of speech is an important right in the United States. Freedom of speech means that you have a right to say you don't like the government, and you won't be punished. It means that you can say what you think and not be afraid.

To keep freedom of speech, we need to practice it. Say what you think. Let other people say what they think. Freedom of speech is important. Keep it alive!

SPELLING TIP

When *i* and *e* appear together in a word, *i* is usually before *e*. But watch out, the exceptions can be tricky!

Practice Book page 62

Practice

Choose a theme and write a persuasive speech.

- What real-life examples might help your audience understand your theme?
- Remember, your purpose is to persuade people to do something or to agree with you.
- Give your speech a beginning, a middle, and an end.
- Read your speech aloud to a partner.

Writing Checklist

✓ Did you state your theme at the beginning of your speech?

✓ Did you use real-life examples?

✓ Did your speech persuade your partner?

125

One Hot Summer in Philadelphia

Vocabulary

One Hot Summer in Philadelphia describes what life was like in Philadelphia during the Constitutional Convention.

Words in Context

1 States sent several **delegates** to represent them at the Constitutional Convention.

2 Shredding papers is one way to keep information **confidential**.

3 Long ago, most houses did not have bathrooms inside. Many people had a **privy** in their backyards.

4 Jane swore Amanda to **secrecy** about the surprise party.

Key Words

delegates

confidential

privy

secrecy

merchants

tailors

cobblestone

curious

⑤ Some **merchants** sell their goods in street markets.

⑥ **Tailors** work hard to make sure people's clothes fit well.

⑦ **Cobblestone** streets seem bumpy compared to most streets today.

⑧ Sam and Sasha were **curious** about the goldfish in the bowl.

Practice

Use each key word in a sentence.

Make Connections

Have you ever visited a historical village or house? What surprised you there? What would you miss from modern life if you were sent back to live in colonial times?

127

The Big Question

Why was life so hard in the early days of our country?

Reading Strategy

Identify Main Idea and Details

The **main idea** of a selection tells you what the story is about. The **details** give you information about the main idea.

- What is this selection about?
- What is the most important thing the author wants to tell you?

One Hot Summer in Philadelphia

by Ann Ponti

Delegates from every state except Rhode Island went to Philadelphia in 1787 for the Constitutional Convention. There were no railroads or airplanes. Some delegates traveled for many days over dirt and cobblestone roads.

The weather was very hot that summer. Men and women dressed more formally in those days. Women wore one or more petticoats under long dresses or skirts. Men often wore suits made of wool. People buttoned their shirts all the way up, even in the summer. There was no air conditioning. People did not take off or loosen their clothing when they were hot.

---

formally dressed up

petticoats long skirts worn under skirts or dresses

Crowds gathered outside Independence Hall in Philadelphia.

It was hard to get medical care in the past.

The meetings in the State House were confidential. It was hot that summer, but the windows were kept closed. Guards kept watch to make sure that no one heard any secrets from the people in the State House. The delegates promised not to tell anyone what happened in their meetings.

The secrecy did not stop people from gathering in front of the State House. They knew important work was taking place. The locked windows and doors made the people curious.

The delegates had to be tough to get through the long, hot summer. If any of the delegates got sick or fainted from the heat, people called a doctor. It was important for the delegates to stay healthy.

Long ago, most people didn't go to the doctor unless they were very sick. There weren't a lot of medicines. People often drank herbal teas to feel better when they were sick. They also made some medicines from plants. Sometimes people didn't get better. Many people died from illnesses that are easy to treat today.

---

tough   able to deal with hard times

fainted   lost consciousness

CheckUp > How did the heat affect people at the convention?

Water sometimes made people sick in the 1780s. People had no way of knowing if their drinking water was clean. To be safe, people didn't drink much plain water. They drank cider, milk, tea, and coffee. They could boil water for tea and coffee.

Houses did not have bathrooms. People used buckets to carry water from nearby wells to their houses. They filled washbowls and pitchers with water to clean their hands and faces. People didn't take baths very often. When they did, they would set a big wooden tub in front of the kitchen fire. After they filled the tub, a whole family would bathe in the same water. The person who went last didn't get very clean!

Like the well, the toilet was outside. It was in a separate building called a privy.

People used washbowls and pitchers to wash their hands and faces.

The 40,000 people who lived in Philadelphia in 1787 had come to the United States from all over the world. People from England and Germany lived next to people from Africa.

People in Philadelphia worked as bakers, teachers, merchants, tailors, and carpenters. They made bread, soap, furniture, and clothing. Their houses were small and close together. Rich people lived in large houses at the ends of the blocks. Poor people lived in houses on the side alleys.

People from all over the world lived as neighbors in Philadelphia.

Bakers and tailors sold their goods from their homes. Farmers used horses and wagons to drive their goods to market from farms around the city.

Life was harder in 1787 than it is today. But the people who lived in Philadelphia witnessed one of the most exciting times in U.S. history.

---

alleys   narrow streets

witnessed   saw

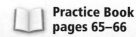
Practice Book pages 65–66

Reading Strategy

Identify Main Idea and Details

- What was the main idea?
- What were some details?
- How did thinking about the main idea and details help you?

Think It Over

1 Why did delegates meet in Philadelphia in 1787?

2 How many people lived in Philadelphia in 1787?

3 Name three kinds of jobs that people in Philadelphia had.

4 Why was water the cause of many health problems?

Phonics & Fluency

Phonics

Consonant Digraphs: *ch, sh,* and *th*

Read the words in the chart aloud. Listen for the sounds of the letters.

ch	sh	th
charm	ship	than
merchants	shut	gathered

Rule Box

The letters *ch* blend together to make one sound. So do the letters *sh* and the letters *th*. These digraphs can be at the beginning, in the middle, or at the end of a word.

Practice

Read the sentences below with a partner.

- List each word with *ch, sh,* or *th*.
- List six other words spelled with *ch, sh,* or *th*.

Facts about Philadelphia

1. Both George and Martha Washington slept there.
2. Many merchant ships docked there.
3. Teachers, butchers, and shoemakers lived there.
4. The Founding Fathers met there.
5. It's the home of cheese steaks and hoagies.

Fluency

Look Ahead

Sometimes readers look for hard words before they read. Then they try to figure them out.

Practice

| Pick one passage. | → | Find any hard words. | → | Practice saying those words. | → | Read the passage aloud. |

1 Life in Philadelphia was hard in 1787. Many delegates had to travel a long way on cobblestone roads. The delegates went to Philadelphia because they had an important job to do.

2 The meetings in the State House were confidential. It was hot that summer, but the windows were kept closed. Some of the windows were nailed shut! Guards kept watch to make sure that no one heard any secrets from the people in the State House.

3 Water sometimes made people sick in the 1780s. People had no way of knowing if their drinking water was clean. To be safe, people didn't drink much plain water. They drank cider, milk, tea, and coffee. They could boil water for tea and coffee.

Houses did not have bathrooms. People used buckets to carry water from nearby wells to their houses. They filled washbowls and pitchers with water to clean their hands and faces. People didn't take baths very often. When they did, they would set a big wooden tub in front of the kitchen fire.

Comprehension

Main Idea and Details

Identifying the **main idea and details** can help you understand what you read. Ask yourself, "What was the reading about?" Your answer to the question is the main idea of the selection.

Practice

Write a sentence about each of the phrases. Then state whether if your sentence tells about a detail or the main idea of the selection.

1. cobblestone roads
2. dirty water
3. hot weather
4. Constitutional Convention
5. closed windows

Use a Main Idea and Details Chart

You can use a Main Idea and Details Chart to help you understand what you read.

Copy this Main Idea and Details Chart. Fill in the chart to show the main idea of the selection and some details that support it.

Main Idea

Supporting Detail

It was very hard to travel to Philadelphia in 1787.

Supporting Detail

Supporting Detail

Extension

Choose one supporting detail from your chart. Write your ideas about how that detail is different today. For example, today it is easy to travel to Philadelphia by car, bus, train, or airplane. Share your work with a partner or group.

Grammar & Writing

Letters

Steve wrote a letter to a teacher to ask her for information about Philadelphia. This is a formal letter.

address — 984 Clearview Avenue
Sunnyville, CA 90012
date — October 20, 2010

salutation — Dear Ms. Johnson,

body
Please send me information about Philadelphia. I am interested in places that are important in the city's early history. I plan to share the information with my class.

Thank you for your help.

closing — Sincerely,

signature — Steve Cho

Practice

Write each item correctly. Use the sample letter as a guide.

1. main street

2. miami fl

3. april 28 2008

4. dear mr singh

5. sincerely

Practice Book page 69

Write a Persuasive Letter

Read this letter from Jake to his friend, Tracy. He wants her to visit Philidelphia. This is an example of a friendly letter.

January 5, 2009

Dear Tracy,

You have to go to Philadelphia. I went on a weekend trip with my family, and it was awesome.

I visited Independence Hall. That is where the Declaration of Independence was written. It was great to imagine myself signing that important piece of paper.

I also ate a cheesesteak. Philadelphia is famous for that messy sandwich. It was delicious! You have to go to there and try it.

Your friend,
Jake

Practice

Write a letter to persuade someone to help you solve a problem.

- Identify yourself and explain what you want.
- Give good reasons why the person should help you.
- Read your letter aloud to a partner.

Writing Checklist

✓ Did your letter explain your point of view?

✓ Did you ask the reader to think about your idea?

✓ Can a partner understand your letter?

Vocabulary

One Out of Many

One Out of Many is about some of the things people discussed at the Constitutional Convention in 1787.

Key Words

surrender

veteran

republic

federal

separate

legislature

Words in Context

1 A white flag is the universal symbol of **surrender**. It means you want to stop fighting.

2 This **veteran** was a soldier in the Vietnam War.

3 George Washington was the first president of the new **republic** called the United States.

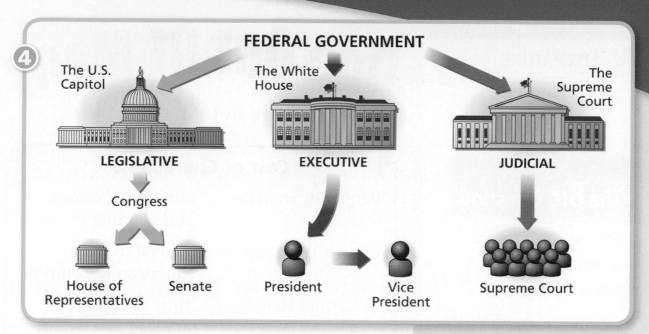

FEDERAL GOVERNMENT

④

The U.S. Capitol — **LEGISLATIVE** → Congress → House of Representatives, Senate

The White House — **EXECUTIVE** → President → Vice President

The Supreme Court — **JUDICIAL** → Supreme Court

④ The United States has a **federal** government that has three **separate** branches: the executive branch, the legislative branch, and the judicial branch.

⑤ The **legislature** of the U.S. government is also called Congress. It has two parts: the Senate and the House of Representatives.

⑤

Practice

Use each key word in a sentence.

Make Connections

Congress has two senators from every state. The number of representatives from each state depends on the number of people in the state. Find out the names of your state's senators and representatives.

Academic Words

convention
formal meeting for a specific purpose

debate
formal discussion

Practice Book pages 71–72

The Big Question

How did we create one country out of many colonies?

Reading Strategy

Make Inferences

You make inferences when you use clues from the story to figure out something that the author doesn't tell you.

- Why was the constitutional convention held in 1787?

One Out Of Many

by Bob McCall

Cast of Characters:

Benjamin Franklin	famous statesman and scientist
George Washington	general in the American Revolution
Alexander Hamilton	army officer and statesman
Bob	boy, 10
Ned	boy, 10

Scene: May, 1787. Philadelphia. Outside the State House. Benjamin Franklin and George Washington are sitting on a bench.

The Pennsylvania State House in 1787.

Franklin: It's too hot, Washington. Make them open the windows in there.

Washington: They don't want rumors to start. (*He sighs.*) This is going to be a very long summer.

Bob and his friend Ned enter. They give the men glasses of water.

Washington: Thank you, Bob.

Franklin: Thanks, Ned.

Bob: General Washington, what is this convention all about?

Washington: It's a kind of meeting.

Ned: But what is the meeting *for*?

Washington: We are here to write a constitution for the United States.

Ned: Oh, a constitution! (*pause*) What's that?

Franklin: A constitution is a set of rules for a government.

Bob: I thought that we already had rules.

Franklin: We do. But they don't work.

Ned: Why not?

Washington: We are the United States. What does the word "united" mean?

Ned: It means "all together."

Washington: How many states do we have, Ned?

Ned: Thirteen.

Washington: It's like we have 13 separate countries. Does that sound united to you?

George Washington was at the convention.

---

rumors　information passed between people that may or may not be true

Check Up　Why did the delegates want to write a constitution?

Bob and Ned: No, sir.

Ned: It's so hot! Why are the windows closed? Do you want to make King George's son the king of the United States? People say that's why the room is closed up tight.

Franklin: Washington, tell the boys we won't let that happen. I told you the windows should be open.

Alexander Hamilton opens the door. He's very upset.

Hamilton: Washington, you must stop Mr. Gerry from talking!

Franklin: That's why we're here, Hamilton, to talk.

Washington: Bob and Ned, this is Alexander Hamilton.

Hamilton: (*stiffly*) Oh. Good day, children.

Ned and Bob: Pleased to meet you!

Hamilton: Gerry says that a federal government will take power from the states.

Franklin: That's true.

Hamilton: But who cares about that?

Franklin: (*laughing*) Mr. Gerry, I guess.

Hamilton groans and goes back into the convention.

Bob: I hope Mr. Gerry talks for a week. I need this job.

Washington: Don't worry, Bob. The convention might last all summer.

Ned: All summer! You really think it will take them that long?

Alexander Hamilton
wanted a strong
federal government.

The British surrendered to George Washington at Yorktown.

Franklin: Yes. People are afraid of government. They think it will take away their liberty.

Ned: We don't want that!

Bob: Make the government weak!

Franklin: What if we have to fight the British again?

Bob: Didn't they surrender?

Washington: Yes. But they might come back.

Ned: We just need a strong army then.

Franklin: Armies cost money. Yesterday, I saw an army veteran in great need. We must take care of the soldiers who fought in the war. France gave us a loan. We should pay them back. Where will we get the money?

Bob: Oh. Is that the only problem?

Franklin: No! There are many things to figure out. But first, we need a strong federal government.

Washington: But not so strong that we lose our freedom. Understand?

---

loan   something, usually money, that is borrowed and then returned

Check Up   What are some reasons for having a strong government?

143

Scene: About three months later. July 1787. Outside the State House.

Ned: What is the new government called?

Franklin: It's called a republic. The people who live in each state vote for representatives to run things. People will elect representatives every two years. The government will have three parts: The first branch is the legislature, or Congress—

Bob: The legislature makes the laws.

Franklin: Right. The second branch is the Supreme Court or judicial branch. This court will tell us what the laws mean if there are any questions. The third branch is the president or executive branch. He will make sure that people follow the laws.

Ned: He's like a king.

Franklin: No. He will only be president for four years. Then people will elect a new president.

Bob: So everything got done after all.

Franklin: There's still a lot to figure out.

Bob: Like what?

---

representatives   people chosen to speak or act for others

Benjamin Franklin was a statesman and scientist.

Franklin: We need a list of rights. People's rights are things the government can't take away, like freedom to say what you think. Then each state has to agree on the list.

Ned: Are you happy with the new government, sir?

Delegates sign the U.S. Constitution.

Franklin: People make governments, Ned. If the people do the right thing, our government will be fine. We still have big problems, such as slavery and rights for women. But you young people will have to figure those things out. We did the best we could.

Ned: Mr. Franklin, you did one very good thing.

Franklin: What was that?

Ned: When you came to Philadelphia, we had 13 separate states. But when you leave, we will have one country.

Franklin: "Out of many, one." That's good. We should put that on a coin.

Reading Strategy

Make Inferences

- Why was the constitutional convention held in 1787?

- Why did the convention divide the government into three parts?

- What helps you make inferences about things the author doesn't tell you about?

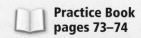

Practice Book pages 73–74

Think It Over

1 Who are the characters in this play?

2 What problems do the characters want to solve?

3 What problems still needed to be solved at the end of the play?

145

Word Analysis & Fluency

Word Analysis

Synonyms and Antonyms

Read these sentences.

> *Washington*: It's like we have 13 **separate** countries.
> Does that sound **united** to you?

The word *separate* means "divided or not joined."
The word *united* means "joined together."
Separate and *united* have opposite meanings.
They are **antonyms.**

Synonyms have the same meaning. What is a synonym
for *separate*?

Word	Synonym Same Meaning	Antonym Opposite Meaning
separate	divided	united

Practice

Give one synonym and one antonym for each underlined word.

1. Ben Franklin suffered from the <u>heat</u>.

2. He complained because the windows
   in the State House were kept <u>closed</u>.

3. Some people at the convention
   wanted a <u>strong</u> federal government.

Fluency

Read with Expression

When you read aloud, use your voice to show feelings.

Practice

| Read silently. | Read aloud. | Get comments. | Read aloud again. |

Ned: He's like a king.

Franklin: No. He will only be president for four years. Then people will elect a new president.

Bob: So everything got done after all.

Franklin: There's still a lot to figure out.

Bob: Like what?

Franklin: We need a list of rights. People's rights are things the government can't take away, like freedom to say what you think. Then each state has to agree on the list.

Ned: Are you happy with the new government, sir?

Franklin: People make governments, Ned. If the people do the right thing, our government will be fine. We still have big problems, such as slavery and rights for women. But you young people will have to figure those things out. We did the best we could.

Ned: Mr. Franklin, you did one very good thing.

Franklin: What was that?

Ned: When you came to Philadelphia, we had 13 separate states. But when you leave, we will have one country.

Franklin: "Out of many, one." That's good. We should put that on a coin.

Comprehension

Make Inferences

When you make inferences, you use what you already know to make guesses about things the author does not directly tell you. Thinking about what you already know will help you make inferences.

Retell

Retell what happened in the play to a partner.

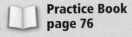 Ask your partner to respond to the Big Question for this reading.

Practice

Tell what you know about the following characters and places in the play.

1. George Washington

2. Benjamin Franklin

3. The United States

4. The 13 colonies

Practice Book page 76

Use a 5 W Chart

You can ask the 5 W Questions to help get information about an event.

Who?   **What?**   **Where?**   **When?**   **Why?**

When you answer these questions, you are giving most of the needed information.

Practice

Copy the Chart. Write a question for each of the 5 Ws. Have a partner answer your questions.

Who?	Who attended the convention?
What?	
Where?	
When?	
Why?	

Extension

With a group, make a time capsule of objects that you would like people to find in the future. Write a description of each object. Present your work to the class.

149

Grammar & Writing

Commas in a Series

Sometimes, you need to list many different people, things, or ideas in a sentence. When you list three or more items in a series, you need to use commas.

Here are two examples of commas used in a series.

Benjamin Franklin, George Washington, and Alexander Hamilton were talking.

They discussed the army, the government, and the king.

The commas separate the items. Notice that one comma comes before the word *and*. You do not use a comma after the last item.

Practice

Write each sentence. Use commas to separate the items in each series.

1. Franklin Washington and Hamilton were in Philadelphia.

2. Philadelphia Boston and New York were three important cities.

3. Pennsylvania Massachusetts and New York were three of the first states.

📖 **Practice Book page 77**

150

Write a Historical Speech

William stood outside the State House during the Constitutional Convention. Here is a speech he might have written. He wanted to persuade people to accept the Constitution.

We must now come together to form a strong government. We need to be able to defend our country. We need a government that can collect taxes and pay for things. We have written a Constitution for this new government, called a republic. The people elect representatives, who make laws. The president serves for only four years. He never will be a king. This new government will protect the rights of its citizens. It will act for the good of all 13 states. I urge you to accept this new Constitution that will make "one out of many."

SPELLING TIP

Some words have silent letters. In words like **might** and **daughter**, the *gh* is silent. You will have to memorize these words.

📖 **Practice Book page 78**

Practice

Write a short speech that a historical person might have made.

- Write one or two points you think the person would want to make.
- Think about the words the person would have used.

Writing Checklist

✓ Did your speech have a beginning, a middle, and an end?

✓ Did you choose a historical theme?

✓ Can a partner understand your speech?

151

The Real Soldier

by Laurie Calkhoven
illustrations by Doris Ettlinger

"Star, someday we'll ride in front of an army, just like General Washington," Jacob said, rubbing the horse's nose.

"You're too young," said his sister Emily.

"I said someday." Jacob was tired of being told he was too young. He and his father believed the colonies should be free from British rule. Two days ago, Jacob and his father had watched the local militia ride by his family's farm. They were called Minutemen.

Jacob wanted to be a soldier. He wanted to join the Minutemen, like his father. His father and other farmers in the area had promised to join General George Washington if he needed help.

152

Jacob was getting some wood to bring into the house when his mother rushed into the barn.

"Redcoats are here," she whispered.

Jacob was scared. He wondered if the British soldiers knew that his father and the other farmers were Minutemen.

Emily was scared, too. She ran and hid in Star's stall. Jacob wanted to hide with her, but his mother needed him. Together, they walked into the yard to face the British soldiers.

Jacob was relieved when he heard what the Redcoats wanted. This time, they only wanted food and supplies.

Jacob chose his words carefully. "My father has gone to the market," he said. "We don't have anything here." Jacob didn't tell the soldiers that the "market" was General Washington's camp!

When Jacob's father got home, he was proud. "Good thinking," he said. "You fooled them."

"I want to help you fight the Redcoats," Jacob said.

"I know," his father said. "But you have work to do here, too. It is important to make sure everything at home looks as if nothing unusual is going on. Your job is to take care of your mother and Emily."

Later that night, Jacob heard a knock at the door. He was scared. What if the British soldiers had come back? He walked slowly to the door.

Jacob opened the door and saw three men. They were carrying guns. Jacob knew the men. They often visited his father. They were some of the Minutemen he had seen two days ago.

"Hi, Jacob," one of the men said.

"My father isn't here," Jacob said.

"We know. Your father said we could meet here. He said you would keep watch and that your mother had food for us."

Jacob kept watch while the men made their plans. Jacob's mother served the men stew and bread.

Jacob listened to their plans, his eyes wide. "May I come with you?" he asked.

"Your job is here," one of the men replied.

"But my father said I was brave today. I can be brave again," Jacob said. "Star is ready for battle, and so am I."

The men laughed.

"What if the Redcoats come back?" one of the men asked. "We need you here." The men grabbed their guns and hats. "Look after your mother and sister," they said as they went out into the night.

There was a loud knock at the door a few hours later.

Jacob opened the door a tiny bit. Two British soldiers pushed the door open and marched into the room.

"Where is your husband?" a soldier shouted to Jacob's mother.

"He went to the market," she said.

Emily held on to her mother's skirts. She hugged her doll tightly.

Jacob knew he had to be brave. He put his hands in his pockets and tried to act calm. He tried to act like a soldier.

"We haven't seen any Minutemen today," Jacob said in a strong voice. Like his mother, he chose his words carefully. The Minutemen left his house a few hours ago.

The soldier narrowed his eyes and stared at Jacob.

Jacob did not move. He looked directly at the man. "British soldiers were here earlier today," he said. "But no Minutemen."

The Redcoats searched the house. They did not find any Minutemen. The Redcoats were angry, but they left. Jacob, Emily, and their mother sighed with relief. They hoped that they would not see any more British soldiers.

The next morning, Jacob's father came home. He said that the British soldiers had been driven out of the area.

"You helped us by fooling the Redcoats," Jacob's father said to him. "We were able to surprise them."

Jacob knew his father had gone to fight the war, but he was a real soldier at home.

UNIT 3 Wrap Up

The Big Question

How do people create new countries?

Written	Oral	Visual/Active
Biography	**Speech**	**Collage**
Research one of the people who helped form our country. Write a short biography of his of her life.	Find the text of a famous speech. Practice reading part of the speech. Then deliver it to the class.	Use drawings, photos, and magazine clippings to create a collage that shows what freedom means to you.
Letter	**Skit**	**Brochure**
Suppose you lived in Philadelphia in 1787. Write a letter to a friend, telling about the events in this unit. Be sure to tell about everyday life, too.	Write and perform a skit about a family during the American Revolution. Include details about the Minutemen, the Redcoats, and people's opinions about King George.	Design a brochure that tells about the historical sites in Philadelphia. Include illustrations and captions.
Report	**Presentation**	**Diorama**
Learn more about the Constitutional Convention. Choose one topic and write a short report about it.	Work as a group. Create a program that explains one feature of the new U.S. government. Present your program to younger students.	Create a diorama that shows an important scene from U.S. history. Include important people and events in your scene.

✓ Learning Checklist

Word Analysis and Phonics

✓ Pronounce *r*-controlled words that contain *ar*, *or*, and *ore*.

✓ Recognize consonant digraphs *ch, sh,* and *th*.

✓ Use synonyms and antonyms.

Comprehension

✓ Compare and contrast information.

✓ Use a Venn Diagram.

✓ Identify main idea and details.

✓ Use a Main Idea and Details Chart.

✓ Make inferences.

✓ Use a 5W Chart.

Grammar and Writing

✓ Practice subject-verb agreement.

✓ Use correct punctuation and capitalization in letters.

✓ Use commas in a series correctly.

✓ Write a persuasive speech.

✓ Write a persuasive letter.

✓ Write a historical speech.

Self-Evaluation Questions

- How does what you've learned in this unit support what you've learned in social studies class?

- How does what you've learned in this unit relate to the present or the future?

- What grade do you deserve on your project? Why?

⊤ 4 Your Environment

Deserts, mountaintops, tropical rain forests, and grasslands are all places where people live. Animals and plants live in these places, too.

READINGS

① Biomes All Over the World

② Springer Goes Home

③ After the Hurricane

160

The Big Question

How do people and environments affect each other?

LISTENING AND SPEAKING

You will talk about your environment and things you can do to protect it.

WRITING

You will write an expository paragraph about a biome.

Bonus Reading

Marine Food Web

Quick Write

Write several sentences describing one thing you do to protect your environment. Share your work with a partner.

What Do You Know about Your Environment?

Words to Know

1. Use these words to talk about the environment.

 plant

 soil

 wildlife

 insect

 pollution

 energy

---

2. How do you protect the environment?

I protect the environment when I _____ .

 recycle glass

 use trash cans

 ride the train

 plant trees

 conserve water

3. What happens when the environment is protected?

If people _____ , then we will have _____ .

clean air

fresh water

a clean environment

more oxygen *and* **less erosion**

Your Stories about Your Environment

Germany

Bangladesh

Roth

In Germany, we take recycling very seriously. Every city and town has bins where people can bring their used plastic and glass bottles, newspapers, cardboard, and aluminum cans. We hope this will mean a better future for everyone.

Sharma

Air pollution is a big problem in Bangladesh. In large cities, like Dhaka, we are just beginning to measure pollution that comes from cars and factories. We hope modern cars and factories will mean cleaner air for everyone.

João

In Brazil, where I live, rain forests grow along the Amazon River. Rain forests are home to many animals. The trees give off oxygen, which we all need to live. Some people have cut down trees to build homes or have cleared the land for farming. We need to stop cutting down trees. The whole world needs them.

Ama

I live on St. Paul's Island in Alaska. Our rocky beaches get lots of garbage from boats that pass by. We get together and pick up trash, bottles, and cans. In September, children and adults from around the world do the same thing. It's called the International Coastal Cleanup.

What about you?

1 What have you done to help your environment?

2 How are these students' stories similar to yours?

3 Do you have your own stories about how you helped your environment? Tell your story!

Biomes
All Over
the World

Vocabulary

Biomes All Over the World describes the major biomes on Earth.

Words in Context

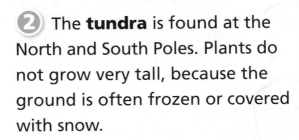

1 The Eden Project in Cornwall, England, has several man-made biomes. A **biome** is a group of plants and animals in a geographic area.

2 The **tundra** is found at the North and South Poles. Plants do not grow very tall, because the ground is often frozen or covered with snow.

3 The **equator** is an imaginary line that runs around the middle of our planet. It divides Earth in half.

4 A **desert** is usually dry and hot.

Key Words

biome

tundra

equator

desert

tropical

grasslands

ocean

5 Most **tropical** rain forests are near the equator. They are usually hot and humid!

6 **Grasslands** are large areas covered with grasses. Savannas and prairies are two types of grasslands.

7 The **ocean** is the largest biome in the world. Oceans cover more than 70 percent of Earth's surface.

Practice

Use each key word in a sentence.

Make Connections

What kind of biome do you live in? Describe the plants and animals that live around your home.

Academic Words

adapt
change to fit a new situation

classify
put into groups

 Practice Book
pages 81–82

167

INFORMATIONAL TEXT

Science

The Big Question

Why does Earth have so many different biomes?

Reading Strategy

Visualize

Good readers often try to visualize, or see in their minds, what they are reading about.

- Use the descriptions in the text and the photos to create a mental picture of what you read.

Biomes
All Over the World
by Tiayana Markson

A biome is a community where certain kinds of plants and animals live. Earth has more than 30 different kinds of biomes. These photos show the most common ones.

Forests cover about one-third of the land on Earth's surface. Forests are filled with trees and plants. Temperate forests have different seasons. In the winter, these forests can be cold. In the summer, they can be hot. Temperate forests get a lot of sunlight. The Sun helps plants grow.

Many animals live in the forest. These animals need to be able to live in different seasons. Small animals, such as squirrels and skunks, can be found in the temperate forest. Large animals, such as black bears, also make their homes there.

community   group that lives together in the same place

temperate   never very hot or very cold

seasons   changes in weather that happen annually

This tropical rain forest is located in South America.

Another kind of forest is the tropical rain forest. Tropical rain forests are in areas near the equator. All rain forests get a lot of rain every year. The rain helps plants grow. In fact, rain forests have more kinds of plants than any other biome. The trees grow so well that very little sunlight can get through the canopy of leaves. This makes the ground in the rain forest wet and dark.

The darkness inside the rain forest makes it a perfect home for animals such as bats and small insects. Many exotic birds, reptiles, and mammals live in rain forests.

---

canopy   cover

exotic   unusual and exciting

Check Up What do trees in the tropical rain forest look like?

The arctic tundra is the coldest biome on Earth. Trees do not grow in the tundra. Winds are very strong. Ice covers the ground, and water freezes. Animals such as polar bears must be able to live in the cold. Most animals that live in the tundra have extra fat to keep them warm. Many birds and other animals migrate, or move, to a warmer climate for the winter.

In the summer, the weather is warm enough in the tundra for things to grow. Plants and flowers appear. These plants and flowers can live in colder temperatures. Animals that eat plants and grass can find more food during the summer.

---

arctic   very cold

climate   typical weather in an area

Flowers appear on the tundra in the warmer months.

Polar bears like the snow and cold weather in the tundra.

Mountains are on every continent on Earth. Most mountains have forests at the bottom of them. The higher you go up a mountain, the colder and windier it gets. The tops of very high mountains look like the tundra. Only small plants and flowers grow in these areas. The plants usually grow close to the ground, so the wind cannot knock them over. Animals that live on mountains, such as mountain goats and mountain lions, must be strong climbers.

Desert biomes have very little rain. Most plants cannot grow there. Deserts are either very hot or very cold. These climates make it hard for anything to live there. Plants and animals that live in the desert have adapted to live with very little water.

---

continent   one of the main masses of land on Earth

The tops of many tall mountains are very cold and snowy.

Very little grass grows in the desert.

Check Up   What kind of climate does the tundra have?

Bison eat in this grassland in South Dakota.

Grasslands, like deserts, get very little rain. The plants and animals that live on grasslands do not need a lot of water. Enough rain falls to help grasses and some plants grow. They have rain in the summer, but they do not have rain in the winter.

Animals such as zebras and buffalo live on savannas. Many small animals and insects also make their homes on grasslands.

Prairies and savannas are two types of grasslands. Savannas are located near the equator. Prairies are in more temperate areas. Many small animals and insects also make their homes on grasslands. Large animals, like bison, elephants, and zebra, live in grasslands, too.

People have turned most prairies into farms. The soil is good for planting crops. Farm animals can graze on the grass. But this means that there are not as many grasslands on Earth as there used to be.

---

crops   plants grown by a farmer and used for food

graze   feed on grass

The ocean biome is the largest biome on Earth. Oceans are huge bodies of water. They make up 70 percent of Earth's surface. Many kinds of animals and plants live in oceans. Fish, crabs, and clams spend their lives under water. Larger animals, such as whales, sharks, and dolphins, also live in the ocean. Blue whales live in the ocean. They are the largest known mammals on Earth. Ocean water is very salty. Animals that live in the ocean must be able to drink salt water.

Earth has many different biomes with a variety of plants and animals. Look around you. Which biome is most like the place where you live?

A scuba diver goes underwater to explore the ocean.

Practice Book
pages 83–84

Reading Strategy

Visualize

- What did you see in your mind about the desert?
- What did you visualize about the tropical rain forest?
- How did visualizing as you read help you understand the selection?

Think It Over

1 What is a biome?

2 Describe three different biomes.

3 What kinds of plants and animals live in your biome?

4 How do plants and animals adapt to different biomes?

A Closer Look at...

Animals
and Their Biomes

▲ Temperate Forest

Squirrels are one of the many kinds of animals that live in temperate forests.

▲ Desert

This roadrunner lives in the desert. It had to run very fast to catch its dinner!

▲ Tundra

The arctic fox lives in the tundra. Its fur coat changes color with the seasons.

▲ Mountain

These llamas live in the Andes Mountains. Some llamas are wild, but people in the Andes also raise llamas for their fur and meat.

▲ **Tropical Rain Forest**

This poison arrow frog lives in the tropical rain forests of South America.

▲ **Ocean**

Sharks live in the ocean. They are an important part of the marine food web.

◀ **Savanna**

The rhinoceros is one of many animals that live on the savanna. People hunt rhinoceroses for their meat and horns.

▲ **Prairie**

Prairie dogs are very social animals. They live in underground burrows called towns.

Activity to Do!

These pages use pictures and words to tell about animals and biomes.

- Pick any animal that interests you.
- Research that animal and its biome.
- Create two pages, using pictures and words, to describe that animal and its biome.

175

Phonics & Fluency

Phonics

Final sound: *s, z*

Read these words that end in *s*.

> **mountains**   **biomes**   **pages**   **tops**

What is the final *s* sound of each word?

Rule Box

Voiceless **s** sounds like a snake hissing, sssss. Voiced **s** sounds like *z*. Think of the sound a bee makes, buzzz.

Practice

Work with a partner.

- Read each word aloud.
- Tell whether the final *s* sounds like *s* or *z*.

1. class   **6.** faxes

2. rings   **7.** pages

3. mixes   **8.** goes

4. was   **9.** walks

5. always

Practice Book

page 85

176

Fluency

Look Ahead

Sometimes readers look for hard words before they read. They then try to figure them out.

Practice

Pick one passage.	Find any hard words.	Practice saying those words.	Read the passage aloud.

1. A biome is a community where certain kinds of plants and animals live. Earth has more than 30 different kinds of biomes. The most common biomes are tropical rain forests, tundra, mountains, grasslands, deserts, and oceans.

2. Mountains are on every continent on Earth. Most mountains have forests at the bottom of them. The higher you go up a mountain, the colder and windier it gets. The tops of very high mountains look like the tundra. Only small plants and flowers grow in these areas.

3. The ocean biome is the largest biome on Earth. Oceans are huge bodies of water. They make up 70 percent of Earth's surface. Many kinds of animals and plants live in oceans. Fish, crabs, and clams spend their lives under water. Larger animals, such as whales, sharks, and dolphins, also live in the ocean. Blue whales live in the ocean. They are the largest known mammals on Earth.

Comprehension

Visualize

Writers use words to help readers visualize what they are reading about. As you read, look for words that describe. These words will help you visualize what you are reading about.

Learning Strategy

Take Notes

Take notes on the different biomes. Share your notes with a partner.

? Ask your partner to respond to the Big Question for this reading.

Practice

Describe an object, a person, or a place to a partner by telling only a few details.

- Have your partner guess what you are describing.
- After your partner guesses the object, ask your partner to tell which details helped the most.
- Switch roles.

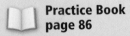
Practice Book page 86

178

Use a Compare and Contrast Chart

When you **compare**, you tell how two or more things are similar. When you **contrast**, you tell how two or more things are different. You can use a T-Chart like this one to help you identify things that are alike and different.

Practice

Copy this chart. Compare and contrast the desert and grassland biomes. One example has been given.

How grasslands and deserts are similar	How grasslands and deserts are different
Both deserts and grass lands get very little water.	

Extension

Make a brochure that shows things people need when they visit your biome. Use photos or drawings to show the items. Write a brief description of each item and explain why you chose it. Show your brochure to the class.

179

Grammar & Writing

Conjunctions and Transitions

Conjunctions join two related sentences together to form a compound sentence.

> Ice covers the ground, **and** water freezes in the tundra.

Transitions show a change in ideas from one sentence to another.

> Grasslands, like deserts, get very little rain. **But** enough rain falls to help grasses and some plants grow.

Practice

Read the sentences. Tell whether *and* or *but* are conjunctions or transitions.

1. Many kinds of plants grow in a forest, and many kinds of animals live there.

2. Most of the animals, such as squirrels and chipmunks, are small. But larger animals also live in forests.

3. Oceans are huge bodies of water, and they make up 70 percent of Earth's surface.

4. Some animals that live in the ocean eat plants, and some hunt other animals for food.

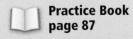

**Practice Book
page 87**

Write an Expository Paragraph

Expository writing answers a question or explains
something. Read Yukiko's answer to a science question.

Why are there no
trees on mountaintops?
Trees cannot live
on mountaintops. The
weather is too cold.
Lower down, mountains do have trees.
But as you go up a mountain, the air gets colder
and windier. As you go higher, only small plants,
grasses, and flowers can grow. No plants can
grow at the very tops of mountains.

Practice

**Write a paragraph that explains one
feature of a biome.**

- Think of a question to answer or
  decide what you want to explain.
- What is the most important thing
  you want to say? Write that.
- Write facts that support that
  statement.

SPELLING TIP

When a one-syllable
word ends with a
short vowel and
the /ch/ sound, that
sound is spelled
ch or *tch*. Check a
dictionary to get the
correct spelling.

 **Practice Book
page 88**

Writing Checklist

✔ Did you answer a question
or explain something about
a biome?

✔ Did you support your answer
with facts from the selection?

✔ Can a partner understand
your paragraph?

Springer Goes Home

Vocabulary

Springer Goes Home is about an orca, or killer whale, who is reunited with her pod.

Key Words

pods

orphan

migrated

predator

reunite

starvation

Words in Context

1 Groups of the same kind of animal have special names. Groups of orcas, or killer whales, are called **pods**.

2 This elephant has lost its mother. It is an **orphan**.

3 These geese **migrated** to their spring breeding grounds.

4 An owl is a **predator**. It hunts at night for mice and other small animals.

5 Tom was happy to **reunite** with his dog, Max.

6 These people are giving away food so that others don't suffer from **starvation**.

Practice

Use each key word in a sentence.

Make Connections

If you find a wild animal that is an orphan, should you try to help it? Why or why not?

Academic Words

consume
eat

goal
something you want to achieve

📖 **Practice Book pages 89–90**

183

INFORMATIONAL TEXT

Magazine Article

The **Big** Question

How can humans protect wild animals in their environment?

Reading Strategy

Make Predictions

- Read the title.
- Look at the pictures and read the captions.
- Read the words and definitions at the bottom of the page.
- Read the first and last paragraph.
- Predict what the selection is about.

Springer Goes Home

by Matt Kachur

People traveling to work on the ferry in Puget Sound, near Seattle, Washington, got a surprise one morning in 2002. A baby orca was swimming alone in the water. Orcas are sometimes called killer whales. They are not whales at all. They are dolphins.

People were delighted to watch the baby orca. She played with floating logs and rubbed against boats. They called her Springer. Scientists gave her the name A-73. They were very concerned. Orcas live in family groups called pods. It is rare to see an orca traveling alone. Scientists also worried about Springer's smell because they thought she might be starving to death. Mammals, like Springer, sometimes have bad breath when they are breaking down their own body fat instead of eating.

---

delighted   very pleased
concerned   worried

Scientists could tell which pod Springer belonged to by the sounds she made. The scientists believed Springer's mother died in 2000, leaving her an orphan.

After six months, scientists had to decide what to do with Springer. They had three choices. First, they could leave Springer alone. They were afraid she would face starvation. Second, the scientists could capture Springer. They could bring her to a marine park to live. She would be well taken care of in a marine park, but scientists thought she would be unhappy. Third, scientists could try to reunite Springer with her pod.

Scientists and environmentalists both liked the third idea. No one had ever reunited an orca with its pod before. What would happen to Springer if her pod did not accept her? Scientists and environmentalists also knew that Springer could be hurt or killed when they tried to capture her.

---

capture   catch

environmentalists   people concerned about the environment

Orcas, or killer whales, usually live in groups called pods.

CheckUp   How will the scientists try to help Springer?

Springer gets medical attention in her net pen.

Scientists decided to reunite Springer with her pod. They acted quickly. Springer was already rubbing against boats in Puget Sound. It was easy for scientists to coax Springer into letting them touch her and put a net around her. Then they lifted Springer onto a barge. They transported her to a special net pen where she would have freedom to swim, and scientists could care for her.

Scientists examined Springer. They found she was starving. Her skin had many open sores. Scientists fed Springer salmon that had been treated with antibiotics. They fed Springer through a tube so she would not learn to connect the scientists with her food.

Springer lived in the net pen for about a month. When she was healthy and eating enough food, it was time to take her to her pod.

coax   gently persuade

examined   studied something to find out more about it

antibiotics   drugs that kill bacteria and cure infections

BRITISH COLUMBIA

Vancouver CANADA

U.S.

PACIFIC OCEAN

Seattle

WASHINGTON

OREGON

Orcas are predators. They eat other animals. Scientists knew that Springer's pod had migrated to a place near British Columbia to feed on salmon.

Scientists took Springer to the area where her pod was feeding. They placed microphones in the water to try to hear the calls of her pod. It wasn't long before Springer heard the squeaks and squeals of her pod. She got very excited!

The scientists put a monitoring device on Springer so they could check on her health. They set her free the next morning.

The next summer, scientists were happy to see Springer swimming with her pod. They believe a relative taught her how to hunt and stay away from boats.

Practice Book pages 91–92

Reading Strategy

Make Predictions

- Were your predictions about this reading correct?
- Did making predictions help you to understand the story? How?

Think It Over

1 Why was Springer swimming alone?

2 What decisions did the scientists need to make about Springer?

3 How did the reading end?

4 Describe how the scientists helped Springer.

187

Phonics & Fluency

Phonics

Consonant Clusters

Read the words in the chart. Pay attention to the beginning consonant sounds.

r-blends	*l*-blends	*s*-blends
bring	black	skin
free	floating	spectator
predator	pleased	swim

Rule Box

When **r**, **l**, or **s** come together with another consonant at the beginning of a word, the sounds of both letters usually blend together.

Practice

1. Read the first paragraph on page 187. Make a list of any *r*-blends, *l*-blends, and *s*-blends that you find.

2. Use the words in the box above to answer these clues.

    a. This word begins with an *r*-blend. It's an animal that hunts other animals.

    b. This word begins with an *l*-blend. It means "resting on top of water."

    c. This word begins with an *s*-blend. It's someone who watches something.

    d. This word begins with an *s*-blend. It's something to do in hot weather.

Fluency

Read with Expression

When you read aloud, use your voice to show feelings.

Practice

| Read silently. | → | Read aloud. | → | Get comments. | → | Read aloud again. |

Orcas are predators. They eat other animals. Scientists knew that Springer's pod had migrated to a place near British Columbia to feed on salmon.

Scientists took Springer to the area where her pod was feeding. They placed microphones in the water to try to hear the calls of her pod. It wasn't long before Springer heard the squeaks and squeals of her pod. She got very excited!

The scientists put a monitoring device on Springer so they could check on her health. They set her free the next morning.

The next summer, scientists were happy to see Springer swimming with her pod. They believe a relative taught her how to hunt and to stay away from boats.

Comprehension

Problem and Solution

The **problem** is the main conflict the characters face. The **solution** is how the characters solve the problem.

- What problems did Springer and the scientists have?
- What were some solutions to those problems?
- How were the problems solved?

Practice

These problems are posed as questions. Write a solution for each.

1. How did scientists know which pod was Springer's pod?

2. How did scientists help Springer find her pod?

3. How could scientists tell if Springer was healthy?

4. How did scientists keep track of Springer?

📖 **Practice Book page 94**

Use a Problem and Solution Chart

You can use a Problem and Solution Chart to help you record problems and solutions as you read.

Copy this Problem and Solution Chart. Show the main problems and solutions in *Springer Goes Home*.

Problem

Who? _____

What? _____

Why? _____

Solution

Who? _____

What? _____

Why? _____

Result

_____

_____

_____

Extension

Find a problem in your classroom. Work with a group to come up with different solutions. Decide which one is best. Present the problem and your solution to the class.

Grammar & Writing

Complete and Incomplete Sentences

Look at each group of words.

> People traveling to work near Seattle
>
> People traveling to work near Seattle got a surprise one morning.

The first group of words describes some people. It does not tell what they did. It does not express a complete thought, so it is not a complete sentence. It is **incomplete**.

The second group of words tells what the people did. It expresses a complete thought, so it is a **complete** sentence.

Practice

Read each group of words. If the words make a complete sentence, write *Complete Sentence*. If it is not a complete sentence, add words to make it complete.

1. A baby orca.

2. Scientists saw a baby orca.

3. People in the area called her Springer.

4. Swimming with boats.

Practice Book page 95

192

Write an Explanation

Katrinka thought of one decision scientists made about Springer. She reread the text to find facts. Then she wrote an explanation.

> Why did scientists decide to help Springer? They watched her carefully for a long time. First, they saw that she was swimming alone. The scientists knew that orcas usually travel in pods. They could tell Springer was a baby. She probably didn't know how to take care of herself. Next, Springer didn't smell right. The scientists thought it might mean she was starving. They were also afraid Springer might get hurt or killed by a passing boat. She needed help!

SPELLING TIP

You can simply add *-ed* or *-ing* to many one-syllable verbs. However, with some one-syllable verbs, you will need to double the final consonant, as in *swimming*.

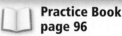 **Practice Book page 96**

Practice

Think about a time when you had to make an important decision. Tell about the decision you had to make. Write about some of the choices you had. Then write to explain your decision.

Writing Checklist

✓ Did you identify the problem?

✓ Did you write about the choices you had?

✓ Can a partner understand why you made your decision?

Vocabulary

After the Hurricane describes how people recover from hurricanes and other big storms.

Words in Context

1 Volunteers gave **assistance**. They helped people find food, housing, and first aid.

2 The worker at the emergency center could not **handle** all the calls that came in during the storm.

3 The flood caused a lot of **damage** inside the house.

Key Words

assistance

handle

damage

stranded

relief

4 During the flood, many people were **stranded** in trees or on rooftops, with no way to get to safety.

5 The volunteers handed out **relief** supplies, including soap, toothpaste, toothbrushes, and food.

Practice

Use each key word in a sentence.

Make Connections

Have you ever been in a bad storm? What happened? Was there any damage? What did you do to clean up after the storm?

Academic Words

authorities
people who are in charge of an area

establish
bring into existence

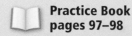

Practice Book
pages 97–98

INFORMATIONAL TEXT

Social Studies

The Big Question

How does a community recover from an environmental disaster?

Reading Strategy

Ask Questions

Good readers ask themselves questions as they read. Here are some questions to consider:

- What are you learning?
- What are you having trouble understanding?
- What are you wondering about?
- What other questions do you have?

After the Hurricane

by Ryan Hunter

When a hurricane happens, it may seem like you are in a very bad rainstorm. Hurricanes are severe tropical storms. They form in the southern Atlantic Ocean, the Caribbean Sea, the Gulf of Mexico, and the eastern Pacific Ocean.

Hurricanes form when winds mix with warm water to make energy. The winds begin to move in a circle. The center of the storm is called an eye, which is a very calm place. As the energy builds, the hurricane grows bigger and more dangerous.

Hurricanes get stronger when they are over the water. Sometimes, hurricanes make big waves. Hurricanes lose energy when they move over land. But the waves might crash onto land and destroy nearby homes.

---

rainstorm sudden, heavy downpour

energy power

destroy damage something so badly it cannot be fixed

Hurricanes may cause great damage. Sometimes, the strong winds pick up cars or street signs. People who live near the ocean have the hardest time during a hurricane. Big waves and heavy rain can knock down or damage things. Hurricanes can cause floods that destroy homes and cars.

Hurricanes often leave people stranded. Cars might not work. This makes it hard for people to get out of the area. People who can help might not be able to get into the area. Cars and trucks break down because of the wind and water. This makes it hard for rescue workers to get supplies into an area where they can help people.

Hurricanes usually begin over oceans and then move to land.

---

floods   large amounts of water that cover an area

break down   stop working

CheckUp   What kinds of help do people need after a hurricane?

197

People might need firefighters or the police to help them during a hurricane.

In an emergency, people in the damaged towns cannot handle all the work that needs to be done. They need help rebuilding homes and roads. They also need basic things, such as food and water. People come from all over to offer assistance. They do what they can to help.

Firefighters and police come quickly. These people go into dangerous places to make sure that everyone is safe. A firefighter might need to go into a damaged home to make sure that no one is left inside. Streets might be flooded. Rescue workers will need to help people get through the water to safety. The workers must act quickly to help people and save lives.

---

emergency   an unexpected and dangerous event

dangerous   likely to harm or kill

Hurricanes can destroy houses.

This woman has come from far away. She is helping children who lost their homes after a hurricane.

After a hurricane, experts come and assess the towns that were damaged. They call rescue workers to help. They also let others know when more help is needed. People come from nearby and from far away to give relief to those who need it. These people are usually volunteers. They do not get paid for their work. They come because they know that people need help after a hurricane.

Many people lose their homes during hurricanes. These people need to stay someplace, such as a shelter, until they can go home. They might feel sad and scared. Volunteers work to help these people feel better. The volunteers can play with children. They can help people find missing friends or family. Sometimes, people just need to talk to someone about what happened.

---

experts   people with special skills and knowledge

CheckUp What work needs to be done after a hurricane?

The American Red Cross helps people after emergencies.

People of all ages need help after a hurricane. People of all ages can offer help as well. Adults might help in towns that were damaged. Young people can make a difference, too.

Some young people try to raise money to send to people who need it. Students at schools might have bake sales or car washes to earn money. They send this money to people who have lost their homes because of a hurricane.

People might donate their own money or money they have raised. Organizations such as the American Red Cross use this money to buy supplies. For example, the money might buy new books for schools that were flooded. Money also helps the Red Cross build shelters where people can stay until their homes are rebuilt.

---

bake sales   events where members of a group sell food to raise money

donate   give something useful to people who need help

supplies   goods that people need or want

People come from other places to help build houses after a hurricane.

There are many ways to help after a hurricane. Think about what people might need if their homes were lost or damaged. People will not have clothes to wear or food to eat. Children will not have books to read or toys to play with. These are all things that can be sent to people after a hurricane.

We cannot stop these scary storms from happening. But we can try to help people after the storms. Even from far away, volunteers can help people whose lives have been changed by a hurricane.

Practice Book
pages 99–100

Reading Strategy

Ask Questions

- What questions did you ask yourself as you read?
- How did asking questions help you understand what you read?

Think It Over

1 What kinds of damage can hurricanes cause?

2 What do experts assess after a hurricane?

3 Why are floods dangerous?

4 Name two things the American Red Cross does in areas affected by a hurricane.

Word Analysis & Fluency

Word Analysis

Homophones

Words that sound the same but have different spellings or meanings are **homophones**.

> - What happens to an area hit **by** a hurricane?
> - The American Red Cross raises money to **buy** supplies.

Practice

Work with a partner. Choose the correct homophone for each sentence.

1. Hurricanes cause (grate, great) damage.

2. Heavy (rain, rein) causes flooding.

3. Many people (knead, need) help.

4. People need clothes to (wear, where).

5. (Some, Sum) need a place to stay.

6. People want (there, their) lives to return to normal.

Fluency

Read for Speed and Accuracy

You should read quickly. But never read so quickly that you lose your understanding.

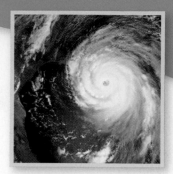

Practice

| Read for one minute. | Count the words you read. | Study any hard words. | Read and count again. |

After a hurricane, experts come and assess the towns	9
that were damaged. They call rescue workers to help. They	19
also let others know when more help is needed. People	29
come from nearby and from far away to give relief to those	41
who need it. These people are usually volunteers. They do	51
not get paid for their work. They come because they know	62
that people need help after a hurricane.	69
Many people lose their homes during hurricanes. These	77
people need to stay someplace, such as a shelter, until they	88
can go home. They might feel sad and scared. Volunteers	98
work to help these people feel better. The volunteers can	108
play with children. They can help people find missing	117
friends or family. Sometimes, people just need to talk to	127
someone about what happened.	131
People of all ages need help after a hurricane. People	141
of all ages can offer help as well. Adults might help in	153
towns that were damaged. Young people can make a	162
difference, too.	164

Comprehension

Sequence

The order in which events take place in a story or a selection is called the **sequence**.

These clues will help you know the sequence.

Signal Words — Look for words such as *first*, *last*, *next*, *before*, and *after*.

Numbers — A writer might include times, days of the week, months, or years to show the sequence. Sometimes numbers show the steps of a process.

Practice

Write a sequence of events for something that happened recently. Use the following sentence starters:

1. First, _____

2. Second, _____

3. Next, _____

4. Last, _____

Use a Sequence Chart

You can use a sequence chart to help you remember what happens first, next, and last in a selection.

Practice

Copy this chart. Complete it to show a sequence of events that occurs after a hurricane strikes.

```
┌─────────────────────────────────────────┐
│ Rain causes flooding.                    │
└─────────────────────────────────────────┘
                    ↓
┌─────────────────────────────────────────┐
│                                          │
└─────────────────────────────────────────┘
                    ↓
┌─────────────────────────────────────────┐
│                                          │
└─────────────────────────────────────────┘
                    ↓
┌─────────────────────────────────────────┐
│                                          │
└─────────────────────────────────────────┘
```

Extension

Work with a group to prepare an emergency kit. (You can use pictures or real objects.) Write a description of each item and explain why your group chose it. Present your emergency kit to the class.

Grammar & Writing

Prepositions

Prepositions are an important link between words in a sentence.

> Hurricanes have high winds that start **over** water.

The preposition *over* links the words *start* and *water* to tell where the winds start. Prepositions often answer questions about where or when.

Practice

Read the sentences with a partner.
List the prepositions.

1. Experts and volunteers arrive after a hurricane.

2. People feel scared during a hurricane.

3. People of all ages can volunteer after a hurricane.

4. Some volunteers play with children in relief centers.

5. Students across the country help, too.

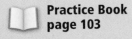 **Practice Book page 103**

206

Make a Poster

Posters give information in short sentences. Sometimes posters use pictures to help the reader understand. Read this poster Sean made.

What to Do After a Storm
Everyone can help!

Rescue Teams
- Search damaged buildings. Look for people who are trapped or stranded.
- Bring them to a safe place, such as a school or other shelter.

Organizations
- Bring food, water, warm clothes, blankets, and toys.
- Help people rebuild or find new homes.

Individuals–What You Can Do
- Raise money to rebuild homes, schools, and businesses.
- Give clothing, toys, and books.

SPELLING TIP

Learn the homophones for common words. Always check your writing to make sure you have used the correct word.

 Practice Book page 104

Practice

Make a poster, with pictures, to tell what people can do to help after a big storm. Make sure your poster is easy to read and grabs the reader's attention.

Writing Checklist

✓ Did you use short, simple sentences?

✓ Were your pictures bold, colorful, and clear?

✓ Can a partner understand your poster?

207

Marine Food Web

by Hiro Ishida

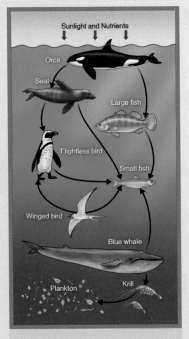

This diagram shows a basic marine food web.

What is the difference between a food chain and a food web? A food chain shows one way that energy travels between producers, consumers, and decomposers. A food web shows many food chains that are connected to one another.

The diagram shows a marine food web. The word *marine* means anything that has to do with the oceans or seas.

Food webs are very important to humans. Any change to one organism in a food web affects all the other organisms in the food web. Natural events, such as hurricanes and earthquakes, cause some major changes to food webs. Humans cause changes to marine food webs by overfishing or pollution. It is important to learn about food webs so that you can help to keep them balanced.

The marine food web starts with the Sun. The Sun gives energy for all life on Earth. Tiny plants called phytoplankton live in water. They capture the Sun's energy and use it to make food. Most phytoplankton cannot move around. They drift in the water. Yet everything in the marine food web that lives depends on them.

Zooplankton are very small animals. They move through the water and eat phytoplankton. This makes zooplankton the second connection in the marine food web. Small jellyfish, worms, and krill are examples of zooplankton.

Many small fish feed on plankton. These fish often swim in schools or groups. This makes it harder for predators to hunt them.

Humpback whales feed on small fish and plankton.

Sharks

Large fish, such as sharks and tuna, eat smaller fish. Other animals that do not spend their entire lives in the water are also part of the marine food web. Penguins and elephant seals also eat fish.

Elephant seal

Penguins

A polar bear and her cub

Killer whale or orca

Polar bears and orcas are at the top of the marine food web. This means they have no predators. They live on fish and other marine mammals.

Decomposers in the marine food web include bacteria and scavengers, such as lobsters. Decomposers eat the waste products of other organisms in the marine food web. They also eat dead animals and plants.

Lobster

UNIT 4 Wrap Up

The Big Question

How do people and environments affect each other?

Written	Oral	Visual/Active
List	**Discussion**	**Poster**
Write a list that shows details about your favorite biome. Include the climate, along with animals and plants that live there.	In small groups, discuss biomes you have visited or have read about. Name some plants and animals that live in each biome.	Create a poster that shows the animals and plants in the biome of your choice. Show how people can help the animals found there.
Log	**Presentation**	**Chart**
List the biomes you have visited or have learned about. Name some of the animals found in each biome. Give details about each climate.	Research an animal in your biome. Make a presentation that explains what the animal looks like, where it lives, what it eats, and its role in a food web.	Make a chart that shows the dangers animals face after a hurricane. Show some ways that people can help bring the animals' lives back to normal.
Magazine Article	**Song**	**Illustration**
Choose a biome. Write a magazine article that explains how people affect animals in that biome. Describe some of the things people can do to help those animals.	Work as a group. Write and perform a song that tells how people can help animals live safely in a biome, such as an ocean or a forest.	You read about a marine food web. Learn about another kind of food web. Create an illustration that shows how the food web's food chains are connected.

✔ Learning Checklist

Word Analysis and Phonics

✔ Distinguish between final *s* and *z* sounds.

✔ Pronounce consonant clusters.

✔ Identify homophones.

Comprehension

✔ Visualize information in a text.

✔ Use a Compare and Contrast Chart.

✔ Identify Problems and Solutions.

✔ Use a Problem and Solution Chart.

✔ Identify a sequence of events.

✔ Use a Sequence Chart.

Grammar and Writing

✔ Use conjunctions and transitions.

✔ Distinguish between complete and incomplete sentences.

✔ Identify prepositions.

✔ Write an expository paragraph.

✔ Write an explanation.

✔ Make a poster.

Self-Evaluation Questions

- How does what you learned in this unit support what you learned in science class?

- How hard was it for you to research a biome?

- What are your strengths in making a presentation?

UNIT 5

Sounds and Music

Playing instruments, listening, singing, and dancing are all ways we can appreciate sounds and music.

READINGS

1

Touching Sound with Evelyn Glennie

2

A Song Map

3

Homemade Music

214

? The Big Question

How do people make and use music?

LISTENING AND SPEAKING

You will talk about the different ways people make music.

WRITING

You will compare two musical instruments and two types of music.

Bonus Reading

The Radio Storm

Quick Write

Write about your favorite kind of music. Why do you like it?

What Do You Know about Sounds and Music?

Words to Know

1. Use these words to talk about music.

 band

 orchestra

 conductor

 notes

 concert

 instruments

---

2. What are some different types of instruments?

A _____ is an instrument.

 violin

 guitar

 drum

 trumpet

 flute

 cello

3. How do you use instruments to make music?

You make music on a _____ *by* _____ .

strumming

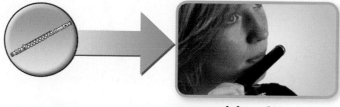

blowing

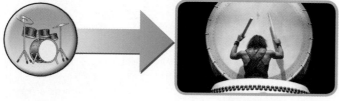

striking

bowing *and* **plucking**

4. Use these words to talk about other instruments.

bagpipes   **bongos**   **tambourine**   **harp**

Your Stories about Sounds and Music

India   Taiwan

Janak

Varanasi, India, is famous for its beautiful music. I am learning to play the *tabla* at school. One drum of the tabla is called the *daya*. It makes high sounds. The *baya* makes low sounds. These drums make the most beautiful sounds in Indian music.

Peiti

I live in Taiwan. My parents play in the orchestra of the Ho-Lo Opera Troupe. In Taiwanese opera, the orchestra is divided into two parts. My mother plays the violin in the part of the orchestra called the *Wen Cheng*. My father plays the drums in the *Wu Cheng*. When I grow up, I hope to join the orchestra, too!

Spain

Bolivia

Inez

I live in Antequera, the heart of flamenco in Spain! I am going to school to be a flamenco singer. I am learning to dance. I am also learning to play the guitar and the *palillos*, or castanets. I want to share the rhythms of flamenco with the world.

Kory

I live in Bolivia. We play our flutes when we celebrate Carnival and other festivals. We carve the flutes carefully from wood. They make such beautiful sounds that people all over the world play them.

What about you?

1 Do you play an instrument?

2 How are these students' stories similar to yours?

3 Do you have stories about music where you are from? Tell your story!

219

Touching Sound with Evelyn Glennie

Vocabulary

Touching Sound with Evelyn Glennie is about a world-famous percussionist.

Words in Context

1 A band is made up of **musicians** playing many different **instruments**.

Key Words

musicians

instruments

percussion

sounds

vibrations

hearing

② **Percussion** instruments make sounds when they are hit, shaken, rubbed, or scraped. Snare and bass drums, cymbals, timpani, and marimbas are percussion instruments.

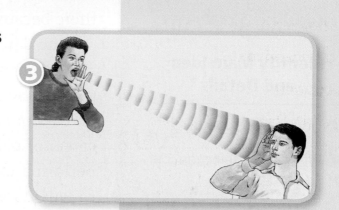

③ **Sounds** travel as **vibrations** in the air. These vibrations are called sound waves. The sound waves enter the ear so you can hear the sounds. **Hearing** is one of the five senses.

Practice

Use each key word in a sentence.

Make Connections

Sit silently for one minute with your eyes closed. Then write a list of the different sounds you heard.

Academic Words

context
situation, events, or information related to something

demonstrate
show

Practice Book pages 107–108

The **Big** Question

How can you hear without using your ears?

Reading Strategy

Identify Main Idea and Details

As you read, ask yourself:

- What is the selection about?
- What is the most important idea?
- What details help support the main idea?

Touching Sound with Evelyn Glennie

by Trish Marx

People walking through Grand Central Station in New York City often hear musicians performing. Musicians like to play there because of the large crowds.

One day, people gathered in the main concourse to hear Evelyn Glennie play her snare drum. She is the first percussionist in the world who made a career of performing as a soloist. Evelyn's performance was filmed for a documentary called *Touch the Sound*. The audience applauded when she finished playing.

Many people watching Evelyn did not know she couldn't hear the music she played. She is almost completely deaf.

---

concourse large hallway

soloist musician who performs alone

documentary movie about real people and events

The marimbas are one of many instruments Evelyn Glennie plays.

Evelyn grew up on a farm in Scotland. There was a piano in her home. As a young child, she asked her parents to let her take piano lessons. They let her take lessons when she was eight years old. Evelyn soon found out she had what musicians call "perfect pitch." She could hear the notes perfectly in her mind. This was good, because she was slowly losing her hearing.

Evelyn found that hearing aids kept her from being able to perceive sounds with the rest of her body. She stopped wearing them when she was 12 years old. Evelyn knew she could hear the correct music notes in her mind. She also used her body to feel the vibrations the instruments made. She learned to play many percussion instruments. This surprised her teachers, who thought Evelyn would not be able to play music once she lost her hearing.

---

perceive   experience

Kettle drums are also called timpani.

Check Up How does Evelyn hear sounds?

Evelyn loved the way music made her feel — sometimes happy, sometimes sad, but always alive.

She studied at the Royal Academy of Music after high school. She has had a successful career as a musician ever since.

On her Web site, Evelyn says, "Hearing is a special form of touch. Deafness does not mean that you can't hear. It only means that there is something wrong with the ears."

Evelyn uses her whole body to feel sounds. She often performs barefoot.

"Anything you can pick can create a sound," says Evelyn.

Evelyn plays well-known percussion instruments such as the snare, kettle, and bass drums. She also plays marimbas, xylophones, gongs, and the water drums pictured below. She has been filmed creating music using common objects, such as plates, pots and pans, bottles, pipes, and glasses filled with water.

---

career   job or profession

These are water drums.

224

Evelyn performs in more than 100 concerts each year. She has won many awards for her music, including several Grammy Awards. These awards recognize high achievement in making and recording music. Evelyn has performed with some of the world's most famous musicians and orchestras. She writes and produces her own music. Many musicians have written compositions for her to play.

When she is not performing or writing music, Evelyn works hard to improve music education in schools in the United Kingdom. She also enjoys riding her motorcycle and making jewelry.

If you are inspired by Evelyn's life and music, learn more about your favorite instrument, and make your own music.

Evelyn performs more than 100 concerts each year.

---

achievement   accomplishment

compositions   pieces of music

inspired   given energy to do something

Practice Book pages 109–110

Reading Strategy

Identify Main Idea and Details

- What is the main idea of the selection?
- What details told you about the main idea?
- How did finding the main idea and details help you understand the selection?

Think It Over

1 What kinds of instruments does Evelyn play?

2 What does perfect pitch mean?

3 What does Evelyn say about hearing?

4 Why did Evelyn win several Grammy Awards?

225

Phonics & Fluency

Phonics

Ending: *-ed*

The ending *-ed* is often part of past tense verbs. Pay attention to how the *-ed* ending is pronounced.

> Evelyn's performance was film**ed** for a documentary call**ed** *Touch the Sound*. The audience applaud**ed** when she finished playing.

The *-ed* in **applauded** is a separate syllable. The *-ed* in **filmed** and **finished** is not a separate syllable.

Why is the *-ed* ending a separate syllable in some words and not in others?

Rule Box

If the letter *d* or the letter *t* comes before the *-ed* ending, then *-ed* is pronounced as a separate syllable.

Practice

Work with a partner. Take turns.

- Write five other words with the ending *-ed*.
- Ask your partner to read each word and tell whether the *-ed* is a separate syllable.

Fluency

Look Ahead

Sometimes readers look for hard words before they read. They then try to figure them out.

Practice

| Pick one passage. | → | Find any hard words. | → | Practice saying those words. | → | Read the passage aloud. |

1 Evelyn Glennie is the world's first solo percussionist. She has never let deafness stop her from playing music. Evelyn travels around the world, playing with many famous musicians and orchestras.

2 One day, people gathered in the main concourse to hear Evelyn Glennie play her snare drum. She is the first percussionist in the world who made a career of performing as a soloist. Evelyn's performance was filmed for a documentary called *Touch the Sound*. The audience applauded when she finished playing.

3 Evelyn found that hearing aids kept her from being able to perceive sounds with the rest of her body. She stopped wearing them when she was 12 years old. Evelyn knew she could hear the correct music notes in her mind. She also used her body to feel the vibrations the instruments made. She learned to play many percussion instruments.

227

Comprehension

Main Idea and Details

The **main idea** is the most important idea in a selection. **Details** give information about the main idea. The details support the main idea by telling important facts.

Learning Strategy

Summarize

Summarize the selection for a partner.

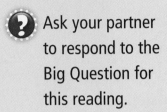 Ask your partner to respond to the Big Question for this reading.

Practice Book

📖 **page 112**

Practice

Read the sentences below.

- Evelyn says hearing is a special form of touch.
- Evelyn could feel the vibrations the instruments made.
- Musicians play in Grand Central Station because of the large crowds.
- Evelyn Glennie's story proves that people can overcome challenges.

1. Which sentence tells the main idea?

2. Which two sentences tell important details to support the main idea?

Use a Main Idea and Details Chart

Writers use details to help explain the main idea. A Main Idea and Details Chart can help you see a writer's plan.

Practice

Copy this Main Idea and Details Chart. Add the main idea from the previous page. Then reread the selection and add at least two more details.

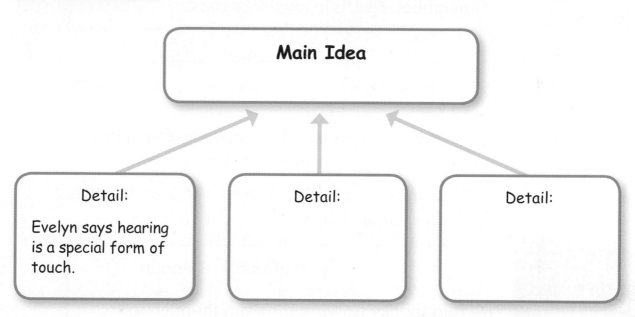

Main Idea

Detail:

Evelyn says hearing is a special form of touch.

Detail:

Detail:

Extension

Make a brochure of different percussion instruments from around the world. Use pictures, photos, and text to describe the instruments. Share your brochure with the class.

Grammar & Writing

Appositives and Prepositional Phrases

An **appositive** is a noun or noun phrase that is placed beside another noun to help explain it.

> My neighbor, **Elsa**, is in my dance class.

Sometimes, an appositive can include more than one word.

> Rocky, **the smallest puppy**, loves to run and play.

A **prepositional phrase** begins with a preposition, such as *after* or *in*, and ends with a noun.

> preposition   noun
> We told spooky stories **during the thunderstorm**.

Practice

Read each sentence. List each appositive. Then list each prepositional phrase.

1. My sister, Bonnie, slept during the trip.

2. A great singer, Alex, won the contest at school.

3. José, my older brother, hid the ball in the bushes.

**Practice Book
page 113**

Write an Introductory Paragraph

When you write a long essay, it is important to write a paragraph that introduces the topic. Muna wrote this paragraph to introduce her essay about two artists in her class.

There are many artists in my class. They use different themes in their art. Today, I am going to write about art made by two of my classmates, Olivia and Ron. Both Olivia and Ron are excellent artists, but their art is very different. Olivia likes to paint scenes of castles, princes, and dragons. Ron uses the same themes in his art, but he draws cartoons. Olivia's art has a long-ago feeling. Ron's art is more modern. Both types of art tell wonderful stories, which I will describe in this essay.

SPELLING TIP

Thinking of a related word will help you spell a word you don't know. For example, remembering **crumble** can help you spell **crumb** correctly.

 Practice Book page 114

Practice

Write an introductory paragraph in which you compare two instruments.

- Give some basic information to introduce your topic, but save the details for paragraphs that will follow.
- Read your paragraph aloud to a partner.

Writing Checklist

✔ Did you indent the first sentence of your paragraph?

✔ Did your paragraph introduce your topic?

✔ Did your paragraph give some basic information?

✔ Can a partner identify the two items you were comparing?

A Song Map

Vocabulary

A Song Map is about a song called *Follow the Drinking Gourd*.

Words in Context

1 The baseball player used a **code** to communicate with his teammates during a game.

2 The boy opened the cage because he thought the bird wanted to **escape**.

3 The big, old tree is one of the well-known **landmarks** in our area.

Key Words

- code
- escape
- landmarks
- secret
- riverbank
- tracks

4 Dan told his friend a **secret**.

5 In spring, wildflowers cover the **riverbank**. They grow right up to the edge of the water.

6 When people or animals walk in the dirt or mud, they leave **tracks**. Can you guess who or what left these tracks?

Practice

Use each key word in a sentence.

Make Connections

Can you make up a secret code? With a partner, pick signals or sounds to use in place of words. Then talk to each other using only your secret code.

Academic Words

assist
help

accompany
go with

 Practice Book
pages 115–116

A Song Map

by Ben McKenzie

The Big Question

What messages can songs carry?

Reading Strategy

Summarize

Summarizing a selection or a song can help you understand it.

- As you read this selection, think about what it is mainly about.

Can a song also be a map? Some people think the song *Follow the Drinking Gourd* was really a secret code. Did the words in the song give instructions to slaves who were trying to escape? Did the song point the slaves toward freedom?

Follow the Drinking Gourd
Stanza 1
**When the sun comes back and the first
 quail calls,
Follow the drinking gourd.
For the old man is waiting for to carry
 you to freedom
If you follow the drinking gourd.**

The Big Dipper is a pattern of stars, or constellation, that points north. Could that be the drinking gourd? The sun comes back in the spring. Quail are birds that begin to call in the spring. Did this stanza tell slaves to leave when spring began and to follow the Big Dipper to the north?

---

instructions directions

In the past, people used gourds to drink water. The Big Dipper looks like a drinking gourd.

Who was the old man waiting to carry them to freedom? Some people believe he was Peg Leg Joe, a former sailor who helped slaves. Peg Leg Joe used a wooden leg.

Chorus
Follow the drinking gourd!
Follow the drinking gourd!
For the old man is waiting for to carry you to freedom
If you follow the drinking gourd.
Stanza 2
The riverbank makes a very good road,
The dead trees will show you the way,
Left foot, peg foot traveling on,
Following the drinking gourd.

Some people say Peg Leg Joe marked trees and other landmarks along the riverbank. This helped the slaves make sure they were going in the right direction. These tracks, or marks, were often a mud or charcoal outline of a human left foot and another mark. Some people believe the other mark was Peg Leg Joe's wooden leg.

---

charcoal   black substance made of burned wood

Check Up › What did the song tell the slaves to do?

Stanza 3

The river ends between two hills,
Follow the drinking gourd.
There's another river on the other side,
Follow the drinking gourd.

As the slaves walked north, they were told to look for the place where the river ends between two hills. Many people think Woodhall Mountain in Mississippi is this landmark.

The Tennessee River is on the other side of the mountain. If slaves kept following the drinking gourd, they went north. They were closer to the states where they could be free.

Slaves found shelter across the river.

(Repeat Chorus)

Stanza 4

Where the great big river
     meets the little river,
Follow the drinking gourd.
The old man is waiting for to
     carry you to freedom,
If you follow the drinking gourd.

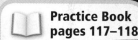

This map shows the directions in which slaves traveled.

The Ohio River is a big river that meets the Tennessee River on the border between Kentucky and Illinois. The song told slaves that the old man was waiting for them on the banks of the Ohio River. Some people believe Peg Leg Joe was there himself to lead the slaves to freedom.

What do you believe? Is *Follow the Drinking Gourd* just a song? Or is it a secret map?

---

border   official line that separates two areas

📖 Practice Book
pages 117–118

Reading Strategy

Summarize

- Summarize the directions in Stanza 2 of *Follow the Drinking Gourd*.
- Summarize the directions in Stanza 4 of the song.
- Did summarizing help you understand what you read? How?

Think It Over

1 What is the Big Dipper? What does it look like?

2 Who was Peg Leg Joe?

3 What clues did slaves get from *Follow the Drinking Gourd*?

4 What was one location identified in the reading?

237

Word Analysis & Fluency

Word Analysis

Figurative Language

Figurative language helps you see in your mind what the author is describing.

> When the sun comes back and the first quail calls, follow the drinking gourd.

The "drinking gourd" is a symbol for the Big Dipper. "When the sun comes back," it is spring, when days begin to get warmer. That line could be rewritten as:

At the first sign of spring, follow the Big Dipper north.

Figurative language does not mean exactly what it says. It paints a word picture.

Practice

Work with a partner. Read each pair of sentences. Tell which sentence creates a better word picture.

1. a. The leaves danced in the wind.
   b. The wind blew the leaves around.

2. a. At night, there are stars in the sky.
   b. The night sky wears a necklace of diamonds.

3. a. The sun provides light for Earth.
   b. The sun lights the world with its flame.

Fluency

Read with Expression

When you read aloud, use your voice to show feelings.

Practice

Read silently.	→	Read aloud.	→	Get comments.	→	Read aloud again.

Stanza 1

When the sun comes back and the first quail calls,
Follow the drinking gourd.
For the old man is waiting for to carry you to freedom
If you follow the drinking gourd.

Chorus

Follow the drinking gourd!
Follow the drinking gourd!
For the old man is waiting for to carry you to freedom
If you follow the drinking gourd.

Comprehension

Make Inferences

The slaves who used the song *Follow the Drinking Gourd* had to make inferences. They put the words of the song together with things they already knew to figure out what the clues meant.

Summarize

Summarize the song for a partner.

 Ask your partner to respond to the Big Question for this reading.

Practice

Write the letter of the inference that can be made from each statement.

> a. The slaves crossed the Tennessee River in winter when it froze.
> b. The song was like a map.
> c. The slaves did not want to be seen.

1. People escaping slavery often traveled at night.

2. The Tennessee River was hard to cross in the summer.

3. The slaves sang the song as they traveled.

Practice Book page 120

Use an Inference Chart

An Inference Chart can help you use what you know to make inferences.

Practice

We often make inferences based on what we hear. Name a sound. Tell what you know about that sound. Make an inference. One has been done for you.

Sound	What I Know	Inference
song playing over microphone	ice cream truck plays that song	ice cream truck is coming

Extension

Find the words to one or more verses of *The Star Spangled Banner*. Discuss the meaning of the words with a partner. Use a visual aid to present your interpretation to the class.

Grammar & Writing

Dependent and Independent Clauses

A **clause** is a group of words that has both a subject and a verb. The verb can be called a **predicate**.

An **independent clause** can stand alone as a sentence. A **dependent clause** has a subject and verb, but it cannot stand alone as a sentence.

> Independent   Dependent
>
> Clay went to the park before he did his homework.

Practice

Copy each sentence. Label each dependent and independent clause.

1. Gael likes applesauce before he goes to bed.

2. When the doorbell rang, we knew it was time to go.

3. Soula stretches before every workout.

4. After going to the movies, Nina and I went home, where we ate lunch.

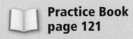

Practice Book page 121

Write a Compare and Contrast Essay

Charlie thought about two different types of music. Read how he compared blues music to rap music.

One of my favorite types of music is blues music. I like the way people sing blues songs, as if they are speaking the melody. The voice is like one of the instruments.

Rap music is very different from blues. It's more spoken. Rap is almost like a drum, with a sharp rhythm that doesn't stop.

Both kinds of music have a lot of feeling in them. The melody seems more important in blues music, and the beat seems more important in rap.

Practice

Compare two types of music.

- Describe each type of music. Write all the adjectives you can think of for each one.
- Discuss the musical instruments each type of music uses.
- First tell how the two types of music are different.
- Then tell how they are similar.

Writing Checklist

✔ Did you use at least two or three adjectives to describe each type of music?

✔ Did you talk about the sound and the feeling in the music?

✔ Can a partner understand your comparison?

Homemade MUSIC

Vocabulary

Homemade Music explains how to make instruments out of household items.

Words in Context

1 You can beat many different **rhythms** on a drum.

2 A **kazoo** is an instrument that's easy to play.

3 Groups of singers often sing different **harmonies**. Some singers may sing high notes. Others sing low notes.

Key Words

rhythms

kazoo

harmonies

flea market

improvisation

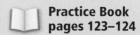

4 You can buy many interesting and unusual things at a **flea market**.

5 **Improvisation** is doing something without having an exact plan. Jazz musicians are good at improvisation.

Academic Words

complexity
quality of being complicated or detailed

variety
difference or range

Practice

Use each key word in a sentence.

Make Connections

Have you ever played an instrument? If you could play any instrument, which one would you choose? Explain your choice.

Practice Book
pages 123–124

INFORMATIONAL TEXT

Music

The Big Question

How do people make musical instruments?

Reading Strategy

Identify Author's Purpose

- Look at the pictures and captions.
- Do you think the author wrote the selection to inform, to persuade, or to entertain?
- Read the selection to see if you are right.

Homemade MUSIC

by Nicky Simser

What do a comb, a washboard, bells, and a glass bottle have in common?

You can make each of them into an instrument. A comb becomes a kazoo. Bells make musical bracelets. A bottle sounds like a **flute** when you blow into it. And washboards? Keep reading to find out! Invite your friends over. You will soon have a band.

People made music long before instruments were invented. They used sticks to beat rhythms. Pieces of wood became whistles. People used objects they found around them every day. It just took some **imagination** to make music.

---

flute   musical instrument shaped like a pipe
imagination   ability to form ideas in your mind

Steel pan drums are made from barrels that once contained oil.

A kazoo is a tube with a hole in the middle. You play a kazoo by singing or humming into one end of the tube. You can use your hand or finger to control how sound moves through the other end. It makes your voice sound different. Kazoos are fun to play. You can make different harmonies with a kazoo.

It is easy to make a kazoo out of a comb. Use any comb. Cut a piece of wax paper. The paper should be twice the size of the comb. Hold the comb with the teeth down. Fold the paper over the comb. Make a crease at the top. Hold the paper close to the sides of the comb, and then sing or hum into the open end. Try not to press on the paper with your lips. When you sing or hum, the paper vibrates against the comb. Does it sound like your voice?

---

crease sharp edge where something has been folded

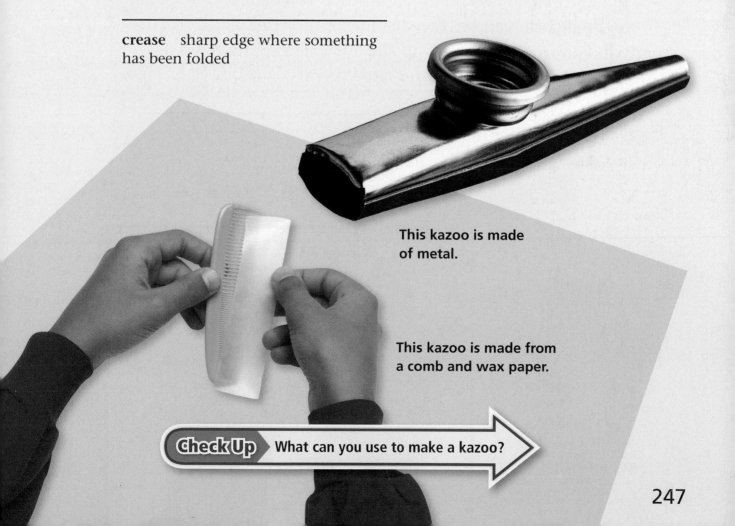

This kazoo is made of metal.

This kazoo is made from a comb and wax paper.

Check Up What can you use to make a kazoo?

Jingle bracelets sound like their name – they jingle! Use thread to tie four or five jingle bells onto an elastic hair band. Leave a space between each bell. Mix the sizes of bells. Each size will have a different sound. Make as many jingle bracelets as you want to wear.

These are Indian jingle bracelets. You can make your own with things from a craft store or flea market.

Practice moving with the bracelets. How do they sound when you shake your arms? How do they sound when you sway your arms? Put the bracelets on your ankles. How do they sound when you march? Do they sound different when you dance?

Jingle bells can be played alone, or they can be part of a band or orchestra. They will add a delicate sound to your group, unless you shake and rattle them!

---

sway move slowly from one side to the other

delicate pleasant and not too strong

You can play in your own band using homemade instruments.

A washboard is a piece of wood or metal with ridges. Many years ago, people used washboards to wash clothes. The ridges helped to get out the dirt. Now, people play music on washboards. You can stroke the ridges with almost anything. Some players use thimbles. Other players use wooden spoons, can openers, or their fingers. Each object will make a different sound. If you go to a local flea market, you may find a washboard!

You have your instruments. Your band is ready to go! Have each of your friends pick an instrument. Let them practice on their own. Then get together and play. Now it is time for some improvisation. Improvisation can also be called jamming. Jam with your friends on your homemade instruments!

Many people play washboards.

---

thimbles   metal or plastic caps used to protect fingers while sewing

📖 **Practice Book pages 125–126**

Reading Strategy

Identify Author's Purpose

- Did this author write to inform, to entertain, or to persuade? Explain.

- How did thinking about the author's purpose help you to understand the selection?

Think It Over

1 What object sounds like a flute when you blow into it?

2 What is the first step in making a kazoo from a comb?

3 What musical instruments can you make using bells?

4 What do some people use to play washboards?

Homemade Instruments

▲ Bells from bottles

Put a different amount of water in each bottle. Then tap on the side of each bottle with a spoon. Soon you will know what sound each bottle makes.

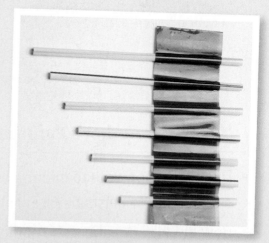

▲ Straw flute

These pan pipes are made from drinking straws and sticky-backed plastic. You can change the pitch of the notes by changing the lengths of the straws.

▲ Cardboard harps

This zither, guitar, and harp are made from cardboard boxes and rubber bands.

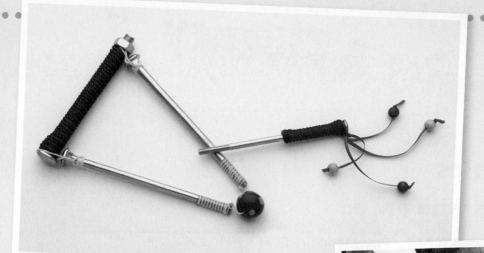

▲ Triangle of nails

The triangle is a popular percussion instrument. This one is made from nails, bolts, and twine.

▼ Bottle flutes

Put your upper lip over your lower one and blow into the bottle. You will hear a sound like a flute.

▲ Spoons

This person is playing spoons. Hit the spoons between your hand and your knee. They will make a clicking sound.

Activity to Do!

- Choose an instrument.
- Find out how to make that instrument.
- Create two pages to tell about that instrument.
- Present your work to the class.

Phonics & Fluency

Phonics

Words with *ow, ou*

Read these words. Pay attention to the vowel sounds.

how	loud	low

Which words have the same letters? Which words have the same vowel sound?

Rule Box

The diphthong /*ou*/ can be spelled as either *ow* or *ou*.
The long /ō/ sound is sometimes spelled with *ow*.

Each word in the chart has the letters *ou* or *ow*. Read the words. If one sound doesn't make sense, try the other.

about	how	owner
amount	know	powerful
around	known	prowl

Practice

Work with a partner. Use the words from the chart.

1. List the words in which *ow* has the long /ō/ sound.

2. List the words in which *ow* or *ou* has the vowel sound in *how*.

3. Add three more words to each list.

Fluency
Read for Speed and Accuracy

You should read quickly. But never read so quickly that you lose your understanding.

Practice

| Read for one minute. | Count the words you read. | Study any hard words. | Read and count again. |

What do a comb, a washboard, bells, and a glass bottle	11
have in common?	14
You can make each of them into an instrument. A	24
comb becomes a kazoo. Bells make musical bracelets.	32
A bottle sounds like a flute when you blow into it. And	44
washboards? Keep reading to find out! Invite your friends	53
over. You will soon have a band.	60
People made music long before instruments were	67
invented. They used sticks to beat rhythms. Pieces of	76
wood became whistles. People used objects they found	84
around them every day. It just took some imagination to	94
make music.	96
Look around you. Do you see anything that could	105
make music? Your hands can. Tap them on a table. Tap	116
a little harder. Tap a little faster. You are making music!	127

Comprehension

Author's Purpose

Authors write to inform or give information to their readers. Authors also write to entertain. Sometimes, authors write to persuade or change the reader's mind.

In *Homemade Music*, the author's purpose was to inform. You learned how people make instruments using everyday objects. The author also informed you about how the instruments are alike and different.

Learning Strategy

Take Notes

Take notes on the different homemade instruments. Share your notes with a partner.

? Ask your partner to respond to the Big Question for this reading.

Practice Book
pages 128

Practice

In the next reading, a class puts on a play. Write sentences about a made-up play. Follow the directions below.

1. Write a sentence to persuade.

2. Write a sentence to inform.

3. Write a sentence to entertain.

Use a Compare and Contrast Chart

A Compare and Contrast Chart can help you tell how instruments are similar and different.

Practice

Reread *Homemade Music* including *A Closer Look*. Complete this Compare and Contrast Chart.

Instruments	Compare	Contrast
spoons and washboard	both are percussion instruments	Spoons make sounds when they are hit. A washboard makes sounds when you rub something on it.

Extension

Find information about your favorite type of music. Make a presentation to the class using samples of music and visual aids. Tell about the history of the music, the kinds of instruments used, and some of the music's performers.

255

Grammar & Writing

Commonly Misused Verbs

Pay attention to the difference between *set* and *sit*.

Set means to place, adjust, or arrange something.
Sit means to rest, or to put your bottom in a chair.

| Please **set** the **plates** on the table. | Please **sit** in that chair. |

Set is a **transitive** verb.
It must act on an object, like *plates*.

Sit is an **intransitive** verb.
It does not need to act on an object.

Rule Box

Transitive verbs have to act on objects. Intransitive verbs never have to act on objects.

Practice

Look up the words *lay* and *lie*. Then complete the sentences below. Look up *raise* and *rise*. Write your own sentences.

1. I am going to ____ on the couch.

2. Anna will ____ the bowls on the table.

3. Do not ____ around doing nothing all afternoon!

Practice Book page 129

256

Write a Descriptive Paragraph

Read how Juanita described a violin.

The violin is made mostly of wood. Most of it is hollow. It has four strings. The violinist holds the violin under the chin and makes sounds by pulling and pushing a bow across the strings. Violinists can also make sounds by plucking the strings. The violin sounds beautiful, almost like a person singing. The violin can play all kinds of music, from classical, to jazz, to rock and roll. I like listening to classical music the best.

Practice

Write a paragraph that describes a musical instrument.

- Choose an instrument.
- Find out what the instrument is made of, what it looks like, how someone plays it, and what kind of sound it makes.
- Read your paragarph aloud to a partner.

SPELLING TIP

Learn to spell words with silent letters and hard spellings by saying them aloud exactly as they are spelled.

tom—or—row

Practice Book page 130

Writing Checklist

✓ Did you use adjectives to describe the instrument?

✓ Did you describe what the instrument looks and sounds like?

✓ Did you describe what the instrument is made of?

✓ Can a partner understand your description?

The Radio Storm

by Zaman Ahmed
illustrated by Jennifer Emery

On Monday morning, Mr. Parker told our class we were going to put on a play.

"There's just one thing," he said. "It must be a radio play."

"A radio play?" Maria asked. "What's that?"

Mr. Parker explained that the play would be a story. We would act out the parts.

"But you won't act on a stage where people can see you," he said. "The radio station will come here to record your play. People at home can listen to your play on their radios."

"You mean they can't see us?" I asked. "Then how will they know what's going on?"

I looked at my best friend, Marco.

"A *radio* play?" I whispered.

The next day, Mr. Parker asked us what we would like our play to be about.

"Remember," he said. "This is a radio play. You need to think of something that has great sound effects."

"Maybe a play about a noisy, galloping horse?" Maria asked.

"Or a play about a rocket ship blasting off?" I asked.

"How about a play with a loud helicopter that makes a whump, whump, whump sound?" asked Bradley.

"Now you're thinking," said Mr. Parker. "Think about things that make noise."

Maria began to tap on her desk. "Here's a galloping horse, Mr. Parker," she said.

Then we all began to make galloping sounds by tapping on our desks.

"Whoa!" said Mr. Parker. "All horses back to the barn!"

We started naming all the noisy things we could think of.

Finally, Mr. Parker said, "Remember, this is going to be a play. That means you need to tell a story, too."

Kaleed raised his hand. "I have an idea for a good story that can be noisy," he said.

"What is it?" Marco asked.

"Okay, it starts like this: It was a dark and stormy night."

"A scary story!" I said. "But can we make storm noises?"

"Easy," said Kaleed. "We wave sheets of metal through the air to make thunder. We all say 'SHHHHHH' at the same time to make the sound of wind. And we can pour water from a watering can to make the sound of rain. We can use coconuts to make the sound of feet running!"

We all loved Kaleed's ideas for the story and the sound effects.

"That sounds like a dark and stormy night to me," said Mr. Parker. "Thank you, Kaleed."

We couldn't wait to perform our play. Mr. Parker let Kaleed choose the sound effect he wanted to make. He said, "I want to make the sound of feet running!"

Kaleed practiced making the sounds of people running. He clapped the coconuts together in different ways. First, he tried tapping them together. Then, he tried tapping them on the table. He liked the way they sounded on the table best. *Clop clop*. The coconuts sounded just like people running.

Maria and I made sounds of thunder by shaking metal sheets. We made the thunder sound like it was crashing right next to us. We all said "SHHHHHH" to make the sound of wind. When it was time for the rain to start, we poured water from the watering can into a bucket. *Splash, split, splat, splash!*

After Marco finished reading the last page of the play, we put down the coconuts, metal sheets, and watering can. But we still heard the sounds of rain and thunder. *Boom! Splash, split, splat, splash!*

We were confused. Then Mr. Parker pointed at the window. There was a real storm outside!

The Big Question

How do people make and use music?

Written	Oral	Visual/Active
Slogans	**Game**	**Demonstration**
Write a few slogans that tell what is good about being able to make music.	With a partner, listen to a piece of music played by an orchestra. Take turns naming instruments that you hear.	Make one of the instruments described in *Homemade Music*. Show a group how the instrument is played.
Outline	**Song**	**Mural**
Skim all the selections in this unit. Look for each musical instrument named. Write an outline that shows each instrument and what it is made of.	Write a song that gives instructions. Use *Follow the Drinking Gourd* as an example. Show your teacher the words. Then perform the song for your class.	Work with a group. Create a mural that shows how slaves might have used the Big Dipper and the song *Follow the Drinking Gourd* to guide them to freedom.
Report	**Radio Play**	**Catalog**
Research and write a report about the life of a musician who faces physical challenges.	With a small group, write and record a radio play. Use some sound effects. Play the recording. Ask listeners to identify the source of each sound.	Make a catalog that shows drawings and descriptions of homemade instruments. Include the instruments you read about and make up some of your own.

✔ Learning Checklist

Word Analysis and Phonics

✔ Identify final *-ed* sounds.

✔ Understand figurative language.

✔ Distinguish between *ow* and *ou* sounds.

Comprehension

✔ Identify the main idea and details.

✔ Use a Main Idea and Details Chart.

✔ Make inferences.

✔ Use an Inference Chart.

✔ Identify author's purpose.

✔ Use a Compare and Contrast Chart.

Grammar and Writing

✔ Use appositives and prepositional phrases.

✔ Distinguish between dependent and independent clauses.

✔ Identify commonly confused verbs.

✔ Write an introductory paragraph.

✔ Write a compare and contrast essay.

✔ Write a descriptive paragraph.

Self-Evaluation Questions

• How have the activities affected your feelings about music?

• How does what you have learned apply to other classes?

• How can you share your interest in music with other students?

UNIT 6

Visiting National Parks

Camping, hiking, exploring, and swimming are all things you can do in a national park.

READINGS

1

Yosemite National Park

2

How to Prepare for a Trip to Yosemite

3

My Trip to Yosemite

The **Big** Question

Why are national parks important?

LISTENING AND SPEAKING

You will talk about a place that you have visited or would like to visit.

WRITING

You will write a research paper about a place you have visited or would like to visit.

Bonus Reading

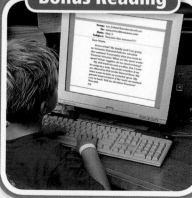

Jay Writes a Research Paper

Quick Write

Write about an interesting place you have seen. Share what you wrote with a partner.

What Do You Know about Visiting a National Park?

Words to Know

1. Use these words to talk about national parks.

 tent

 picnic table

 trail map

 pond

 mountain

 rowboat

---

2. What can you do in a national park?

I can go _____ at a national park.

 camping

 picnicking

 hiking

 climbing

 swimming

 boating

3. What do you need at a national park?

You need a _____ *for* _____ *.*

camping

hiking

climbing

swimming *and* boating

4. Use these words to talk about other things in national parks.

 waterfall

 tourists

 wildflowers

Your Stories about Visiting National Parks

Greenland

Ecuador

Victor

I live in Nuuk, Greenland. Did you know that Greenland is the world's largest island? My country is also home to the Northeast Greenland National Park, the largest national park in the world. The park covers an area of 370,000 square miles. Musk ox, polar bears, and walruses live there.

Amaia

I live in Quito, Ecuador. My government set aside more than a million acres for the Galapagos National Park in 1959. People visit the Galapagos Islands to see birds and animals you can't find anywhere else in the world, such as frigates and giant tortoises.

India

Tanzania

Pooja

I live in India near the Jim Corbett National Park. The park was created more than 70 years ago. The wildlife there includes tigers, elephants, chital, sambar, king cobras, Indian wild boars, hedgehogs, flying foxes, and nearly 600 species of birds. The park helps keep these animals safe from hunters.

Jojo

I live in Tanzania. The Serengeti National Park has one of the most diverse plant and animal collections in the world. These zebras are some of the many migratory animals that make their homes in the Serengeti. People come to study the plants and animals here.

What about you?

1 Which of these national parks would you like to visit? Why?

2 How are these students' stories similar to yours?

3 Have you visited a national park? Tell your story!

Vocabulary

Yosemite National Park

Key Words

- **tributaries**
- **national parks**
- **cliffs**
- **sequoias**
- **grove**

Yosemite National Park describes one of the most popular national parks in the United States.

Words in Context

1 A smaller river that joins a bigger river is called a tributary. The Missouri River has more than 50 **tributaries**. The Missouri River is a tributary of the Mississippi River.

YELLOWSTONE NATIONAL PARK

2 Yellowstone National Park is one of many **national parks** around the world. Is there a national park near where you live?

3 It is exciting to walk along **cliffs**. But, be careful not to walk too close to the edge.

270

4 **Sequoias** are some of the biggest trees in the world.

5 This **grove** of birch trees is in Acadia National Park in Maine.

Practice

Use each key word in a sentence.

Make Connections

What national parks are in your state? If you could visit any national park, which park would you choose? Why?

Academic Words

area
place, geographical region

region
location, large geographic area

 Practice Book pages 133–134

The Big Question

Why is it important to set aside land for national parks?

Reading Strategy

Make Connections

Think about your own life as you read.

- Have you visited places similar to Yosemite National Park?

- What plants and animals look familiar to you?

- Have you ever done any of the activities described in the article?

Yosemite
National Park

by Vivian Ortiz

Whether climbing, camping, or hiking, Yosemite has something for everyone.

The Yosemite region of California takes up almost 1,200 square miles. It is known for its mighty waterfalls, deep valleys, and huge meadows. People have lived in the Yosemite region for 8,000 years. In the 1830s, people from other places visited. Some people built hotels and houses there. Environmentalists worried about this. They feared the land would be ruined.

mighty   very big and amazing

ruined   be spoiled or completely destroyed

The Merced River is a great place to visit any time of the year.

The U.S. government stepped in to help. In 1890, the area became known as Yosemite National Park. Rules make sure the land is preserved for people to enjoy now and in the future. More than three million people visit the park each year.

Yosemite Valley is a popular destination for visitors. It has cliffs and rock forms. Many guests spend time gazing at its waterfalls. Yosemite Valley is open all year. People often travel to the valley by car.

Yosemite National Park is also famous for its trees. Giant sequoias seem to reach the sky. The biggest group of giant sequoias is found in Mariposa Grove. Between November and March, the road to Mariposa Grove is closed to cars because of snow. Can you think of other ways to reach the grove? You can hike or ski!

---

destination   place someone is going to

gazing   looking at something for a long time

Rafting is a fun thing to do on the Merced River.

Check Up ⟩ What can people do at a national park?

Another great place to visit is Yosemite's Glacier Point. It is a high place where visitors can see many of the park's great features. You can see Yosemite Valley. You can see mountains too. Many people go hang gliding there. In winter, you'll need skis or snowshoes to reach it.

Have you ever tried to climb a climbing wall? In Yosemite National Park, people climb real rocks! El Capitan is a 3000-foot high (1000m) vertical rock formation. You can hike to the top of El Capitan on one of the trails in the park. Many people try to climb the face of the cliff itself. Climbing El Capitan is very dangerous. Only experienced rock climbers should try it. It is very difficult for park rangers to rescue climbers who get tired or hurt.

---

vertical   pointing straight up and down

There are easier ways to get to the top of El Capitan!

Hang gliding is popular at Glacier Point.

Yosemite Falls is the seventh highest waterfall in the world.

Yosemite Falls are among the most spectacular waterfalls in the country. The falls are the seventh-highest in the world. The tributaries that form the falls lead to the Merced River. The best time to visit Yosemite Falls is in early spring, when the melting snow really makes the water roar.

The Hetch Hetchy Valley has a funny name, and it's really a fun place! Like Yosemite Valley, it has great views. The Hetch Hetchy Reservoir supplies drinking water to people in San Francisco.

Yosemite National Park is a great vacation place. With all of its great features, there is something for everyone to enjoy.

The natural beauty of Yosemite National Park brings more than three million visitors each year.

---

spectacular   very impressive and exciting

reservoir   where water is stored before it is sent to peoples' homes

Practice Book pages 135–136

Reading Strategy

Make Connections

- Have you visited a national park?
- Which activities in the article have you done? Which activities would you like to do?

Think It Over

1 Where is the biggest group of sequoia trees in Yosemite National Park?

2 Which reservoir supplies drinking water to people in San Francisco?

3 How does El Capitan compare to a climbing wall?

4 Why is it difficult to rescue climbers on El Capitan?

275

Phonics & Fluency

Phonics

Words with *v* and *w*

Read these words aloud. Pay attention
to how your lips move.

vase	verb	was	word

Rule Box

- For words that begin with the letter *v,* narrow your lips,
  and put your teeth against your lower lip.

- For words that begin with a *w,* open your lips slightly.

Practice

Work with a partner. Read the words aloud.

waterfall	were	visit	valley

1. Write three sentences using words with the *v* sound.

2. Write three sentences using words with the *w* sound.

3. Read your sentences aloud to your partner.

Fluency

Look Ahead

Sometimes readers look for hard words before they read. They then try to figure them out.

Practice

| Pick one passage. | → | Find any hard words. | → | Practice saying those words. | → | Read the passage aloud. |

1 Yosemite National Park was created to help protect the land from damage by builders and tourists. Today there are many beautiful places to visit and many fun things to do in the park.

2 People have lived in the Yosemite region for 8,000 years. In the 1830s, people from other places visited. Some people built hotels and houses there. Environmentalists worried about this. They feared the land would be ruined.

3 Yosemite Valley is a popular destination for visitors. It has cliffs and rock forms. Many guests spend time gazing at its waterfalls. Yosemite Valley is open all year. People often travel to the valley by car.

Yosemite is also famous for its trees. Giant sequoias seem to reach the sky. The biggest group of giant sequoias is found in Mariposa Grove. Between November and March, and sometimes April, the road to Mariposa Grove is closed to cars because of snow.

Comprehension

Learning Strategy

Notetaking

Take notes on the features of Yosemite National Park. Share your notes with a partner.

? Ask your partner to respond to the Big Question for this reading.

Connect Text to Self

You can use your experience to help you understand what you read. **Experience** is something that you have done, seen, or taken part in.

As you read, ask yourself these questions:

- How are the people, places, and ideas familiar to you?
- In what ways are they different from your experience?
- How are the feelings described in the selection similar to feelings you have had?

Practice

Think about your last visit to a new place.

- Reread the last paragraph on page 274 and look at the small photo. Think about the feelings created in that paragraph.
- Write about a time when you felt those feelings.

**Practice Book
page 138**

Use a 5W Chart

You can use a 5W Chart to help you ask questions about what you read. If you can answer your 5W questions, you will have a good understanding of the selection.

Practice

Write a question about *Yosemite National Park* in each box.
Then work with a partner to answer your questions.

Who?	Who likes to visit Yosemite National Park?
What?	
Where?	
When?	
Why?	

Extension

Choose a place you have visited or would like to visit. Create a 5W Chart with questions about that place. Try to find the answers to your questions. Then present your chart to the class.

Grammar & Writing

Four Types of Sentences

Writers use different types of sentences to add variety. Notice each sentence has a different type of end punctuation.

> Between November and March the road to Mariposa is closed to cars. Can you think of other ways to reach the grove? You can hike or ski!

There are four types of sentences.

- **Declarative** sentences state something.
- **Interrogative** sentences ask questions.
- **Exclamatory** sentences express strong feelings.
- **Imperative** sentences tell someone to do (or not do) something.

Practice

Tell whether each sentence is *declarative, interrogative, exclamatory,* or *imperative.* Then write your own example sentence for each type.

1. Have you ever tried to climb a climbing wall?

2. Yosemite National Park has cliffs and rock forms.

3. Some people climb that big cliff!

4. Get down from there!

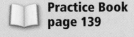
Practice Book page 139

Write a Business Letter

Read the letter Gretchen wrote asking for information about where she wants to go.

Gretchen Koppel
709 Hummingbird Lane
San Francisco, CA 94101

March 7, 2009

Great Smoky Mountains National Park
1420 Little River Road
Gatlinburg, TN 37738

Dear Sir or Madam:

Please send me some information about the Great Smoky Mountains National Park. I would like to know about hiking, camping, and horseback riding. Are there lakes for swimming and boating?

Thank you very much for your help.

Sincerely,
Gretchen Koppel

SPELLING TIP

Learning about prefixes and suffixes will help you be a better speller. For example, the prefix *re* means "again"; *dis* means "not." The suffix *ful* means "full of," and *ness* makes a noun out of an adjective.

 Practice Book page 140

Writing Checklist

✓ Did you include the reader's address and a formal salutation?

✓ Were you specific about the information you want?

✓ Did you use a formal closing?

✓ Can a partner understand your letter?

Practice

Think of a place you would like to visit. Make a list of questions. Then write a letter asking for information.

How to Prepare for a Trip to Yosemite

Vocabulary

How to Prepare for a Trip to Yosemite describes how two friends get ready for a camping trip.

Words in Context

Key Words

- environment
- ecosystem
- alpine
- landslide
- conservation
- secluded
- scenic

1 An **environment** includes the land, water, and air where people, plants, and animals live.

2 An **ecosystem** is part of the environment. It is a community that includes the plants, animals, and insects in a specific area. This wetland is an ecosystem.

3 Things that are high in the mountains can be called **alpine**. Snowboarding is an alpine sport. An alpine lodge is a lodge high in the mountains.

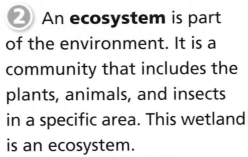

④ A **landslide** destroyed the house and blocked the road.

⑤ There are many ways to practice **conservation**. These students are planting trees.

⑥ Marnie hated crowds. She would rather write on this quiet, **secluded** part of the beach.

⑦ The park had many **scenic** views that people love to photograph.

Practice

Use each key word in a sentence.

Make Connections

When you go on vacation, do you prefer to sleep in a tent, a cabin, or a hotel? Why? What was your favorite vacation?

Academic Words

specific

precise, exact

features

traits, characteristics

 Practice Book pages 141–142

283

FUNCTIONAL WRITING

E-mail

The **Big** Question

What can we learn from visiting national parks?

Reading Strategy

Draw Conclusions

You draw conclusions when you put together clues to figure something out.

- What can you conclude about where Jay lives?
- What can you conclude about where Maria lives?

How to Prepare for a Trip to Yosemite

by Jay Rabin and Maria Reyes

From: Jay_Rabin@lincolnschool.net
To: mreyes@californianet.com
Date: May 5
Subject: Yosemite this summer!!!!!

Dear Maria,

Guess what? My family and I are going to Yosemite National Park for vacation this summer! I remember you went to Yosemite last year. What are the most scenic spots? What supplies do we need to bring?

My dad wants to rent a cabin, but I want to camp in a tent. My mom wonders if we are allowed to fish in the Merced River. My sister wants to hike in secluded spots. My parents want to know if the trails are marked easy or hard. Tell me all about Yosemite!

Your pal,
Jay

vacation   trip you take to another place for pleasure

supplies   food, clothes, and things needed for a particular activity

From: mreyes@californianet.com
To: Jay_Rabin@lincolnschool.net
Subject: Re: Yosemite this summer!!!!!
Date: May 6

Hi Jay,

What great news! You and your family will love Yosemite.

I did go there last year. But I've been to Yosemite many times. I live only a few hours from the park. My family and I go as often as we can.

I will tell you about the spots you really need to see. The first is Yosemite Valley. You will love the waterfalls and cliffs. Don't miss it! If you like giant sequoia trees, you have to go to Mariposa Grove. The best views are at Glacier Point. Long ago, a landslide shaped that part of the park.

Please tell your mom that fishing is allowed in Merced River. Fishing does not disturb the park's ecosystem. There are some rules, but they are clearly posted. They tell where you can fish and the kinds of bait you can use. The trails are marked easy or hard. There are so many trails. Did you decide between renting a cabin or bringing your own tent?

Your friend,
Maria

---

often   regularly or many times

disturb   change something in a bad way

bait   food used to attract fish

 Check Up What do you think Jay will write to Maria about next?

285

From: Jay_Rabin@lincolnschool.net
To: mreyes@californianet.com
Subject: Re: Yosemite this summer!!!!!
Date: June 1

Hi Maria,

I'm sorry I haven't written in a while. My family went on a short camping trip this weekend. We went to the Pocono Mountains in Pennsylvania. We wanted to be sure we have everything we need for our big trip.

Here is a picture of my mom and big sister unloading the car after the trip. They were so organized that it was easy for us to unpack the car. Dad put me right to work on cleaning all the equipment and putting it away.

I convinced my parents to rent a tent when we visit Yosemite. I'm so happy! I think we will have such a good time.

Thanks for the information about places to go. I don't know if I like giant sequoias. I've never seen one. I love to be in the wilderness. I really like alpine trees.

We have a map of the park, a compass, and flashlights. Before we leave, can you tell me what other supplies we should bring?

Thanks, my friend!
Jay

---

convinced   got someone to agree to do something

From: mreyes@californianet.com
To: Jay_Rabin@lincolnschool.net
Subject: Re: Yosemite this summer!!!!!
Date: June 8

Dear Jay,

I bet you can't wait for your trip to Yosemite! I think you will love the environment. I hope you and your family can talk to a park ranger about all the conservation projects there.

It's good that you have lots of supplies already. Don't forget a first-aid kit. Bring extra food, water, and clothes. Your parents should bring a knife and matches. They come in handy for emergencies or for cooking outdoors. Avoid sunburn with sunscreen, a hat, and sunglasses. It's good to have a cell phone, two-way radio, or satellite phone in case you get lost.

Have a wonderful time. Send me a postcard if you can!

Your friend,
Maria

Practice Book
pages 143–144

Reading Strategy

Draw Conclusions

- Why did Jay's family go on a shorter camping trip first?
- What did you conclude about where Jay and Maria live?
- What hints led you to those conclusions?

Think It Over

1 Why is it important to be prepared when you go camping?

2 What supplies will Jay and his family bring?

3 Why did Jay and his family go camping in the Pocono Mountains?

Things You Might Need On a Camping Trip

It is best to be prepared when you go camping. These are things you should bring on any camping trip. If you go camping in winter, bring warm clothing. If you go to the desert, bring extra water.

▲ Sun Protection
- sunglasses
- hat
- sunscreen

▲ Raingear
- rain jacket and pants
- poncho
- boots

▲ Navigation Aids
- map
- compass

▲ Essentials
- emergency shelter
- first aid kit
- flashlight

▲ Nourishment
- GORP (good old raisins and peanuts)
- canteen for water
- dried food

Activity to Do!

- Think of a place you would like to visit.

- Find information about what you need for the trip.

- Create two pages to describe those items.

- Present your work to the class.

Phonics & Fluency

Phonics

Variant vowel: oo

Words with Letters *oo*	
took	too
hook	food

Each word in the chart has the letters *oo*.
Read the words aloud.

What two vowel sounds do the letters *oo* have?

Rule Box

The /o͝o/ sound is the short sound of oo as in **took**.

The /o͞o/ sound is the long sound of oo as in **too**.

If you come across a word you do not know, try reading it both ways. Try the long sound first. It is more common.

Practice

Find each word with the letters *oo*. Sort the words into two lists.

Dear Maria,

Here's a picture of the fish I could not catch. It's a good thing we brought our own food to cook.

I have a crick in my neck from looking up at the redwoods! This place is way cool. We'll be back soon.

Your friend,
Jay

Place Stamp Here

Maria Reyes
10 Brook Lane
Sacramento, CA 94211

Fluency

Read with Expression

When you read aloud, use your voice to show feelings.

Practice

| Read silently. | ▶ | Read aloud. | ▶ | Get comments. | ▶ | Read aloud again. |

Dear Maria,

Guess what? My family and I are going to Yosemite National Park for vacation this summer. I remember you went to Yosemite last year. What are the most scenic spots? What supplies do we need to bring?

My dad wants to stay in a cabin, but I want to camp in a tent. My mom wonders if we are allowed to fish in the Merced River. My sister said she wants to hike in secluded spots. My parents want to know if the trails are marked easy or hard.

Tell me all about Yosemite!

Your pal,
Jay

Comprehension

Draw Conclusions

When you **draw conclusions**, you use the information from the reading to form your own ideas.

- What are some things people worry about when they go camping?
- What do people need to plan for when they go camping?

Summarize

Summarize Jay or Maria's part of the selection for a partner.

? Ask your partner to respond to the Big Question for this reading.

Practice

Read the paragraph. What site did Maria like best in Yosemite National Park? Tell how you reached your conclusion.

> I will tell you about the spots you really need to see. The first is Yosemite Valley. You will love the waterfalls and cliffs. Don't miss it! If you like giant sequoia trees, you have to go to Mariposa Grove. The best views are at Glacier Point. Long ago, a landslide shaped that part of the park.

**Practice Book
page 146**

Use a KWL Chart

You can use a KWL Chart to help you relate your knowledge to the ideas in a selection. The letters stand for "What I Know," "What I Want to Know" and "What I Have Learned".

Practice

Complete this KWL Chart about *How to Prepare for a Trip to Yosemite*. Think back to what you knew before you read and what things you would like to know. Then tell what you learned.

K-What I Know	W-What I Want to Know	L-What I Have Learned

Extension

Work with a group. Choose a place to visit. Have each group member place a picture of an item to take on the trip in a box. You may use the actual item if it is available. Write a brief description of each item to explain why you chose it.

293

Grammar & Writing

Active and Passive Voice

When a verb is in the **active voice**, a person or thing performs an action. These verbs are in active voice.

> You **read** my message correctly.
>
> Long ago, a landslide **shaped** Glacier point.

In **passive voice**, the subject receives the action. These verbs are in the passive voice.

> The hiking trails **are marked** easy or hard.
>
> The rules about fishing **are posted**.

Practice

Tell whether the verb is in the active voice or the passive voice.

1. Three million people visit the park each year.

2. The park was visited by three million people.

3. Visitors catch fish in the lake.

4. The fish were caught by visitors.

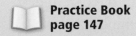
Practice Book page 147

Write a Paragraph in the Active Voice

It is usually better to write sentences in the active voice. Find the active and passive voice sentences in Tami's paragraph.

The Andes Mountains

My parents and I visit our relatives in Peru every year. Our favorite time of year to visit is during Carnival. This holiday period is called Mardi Gras in the United States. The holiday is celebrated by people all over the world. In Peru, we celebrate by having parades and dances. Special food is cooked by families. Some farmers tie ribbons and other decorations to their animals. Everyone has a great time.

SPELLING TIP

You can use your computer's spell check to check your spelling, but the computer can't tell whether you meant **weather** or **whether**, or **your** or **you're**. You must still check your spelling carefully.

Practice Book page 148

Practice

Work with a partner. Rewrite the passive voice sentences in Tami's paragraph in the active voice. Then write your own paragraph about a place you visited.

- Think of a place you have visited.
- Write about something that happened to you there.
- Write your sentences in the active voice.

Writing Checklist

✓ Did you indent the first line of your paragraph?

✓ Did you use the active voice?

✓ Was it easier to write in active voice? Why or why not?

✓ Can a partner understand your paragraph?

My Trip To Yosemite

Vocabulary

My Trip to Yosemite is about Jay's summer trip to Yosemite National Park.

Words in Context

Key Words

- cascade
- meadow
- peak
- ascend
- forest
- valley

1 I love to watch the water **cascade** down the steps.

2 A **meadow** in summer is one of the prettiest places to be. The grass is tall, and the flowers smell sweet.

3 Sometimes, the **peak** of a high mountain stays covered with snow, even in summer.

4 When you **ascend** to the top of a mountain, climbing the last few feet can be the most exciting.

5 It is often cool and dark in the **forest**, even on a warm summer day. The shade from all the tall trees keeps it cool and comfortable.

6 A **valley** often forms between mountains.

Practice

Use each key word in a sentence.

Make Connections

Have you ever watched people climb mountains, go scuba diving, or explore the arctic? Have you seen them on television or in a movie? Talk about whether you would like to do one of those activities.

Academic Words

comment
talk about; say something about

correspond
write messages to other people

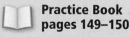

Practice Book
pages 149–150

The **Big** Question

How could you share what you experienced at a national park with others?

Reading Strategy

Review and Retell

When you review and retell a selection, you pay attention to the major events. As you read:

- Ask yourself the 5W questions to help you remember the most important events.

My Trip To Yosemite

by Jay Rabin

Hey Maria,

Check out my cool Yosemite scrapbook! I am going to show it to my friends at school.

Your friend,
Jay

Half Dome is one of the most famous mountains in Yosemite National Park.

August 7

On our first day, we drove to Glacier Point. Our goal was to ascend to the very top. We had a great view from there. We saw a huge waterfall. We could see Yosemite Valley at the bottom. There were so many trees in the valley! We saw Half Dome mountain. It looks like the top of a circle. We passed rock climbers on the way down. People come from all over the world to climb rocks in Yosemite. It looked fun but also a little scary!

We saw these rock climbers. Yikes!

298

Yosemite Valley is one of the most popular places in Yosemite National Park.

Merced River is where visitors swim. People also go rafting down the river.

August 9

The next day we saw Yosemite Valley again. This time we saw it from the ground. We took a 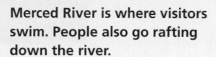mule ride through the valley. Riding the mule was fun, but bumpy. I was sore afterwards! Many people go on mule tours in Yosemite. There are trees and grass everywhere. We rode to Mirror Lake. When it is filled with water you can see the reflections of mountains in it, like a mirror. We learned that the lake is slowly turning into a meadow. There is not much water there anymore. It is mostly grass and plants. The lake was pretty, but the meadow is, too.

Later we went to a long river called Merced River. The edge of the river is like a beach. Many families sat on the sand. We swam in the water. We also watched some people go rafting.

---

mule   a cross between a horse and a donkey

tours   short trips through a place to see it

Check Up ▸ What did Jay's family do on August 9?

August 10

We wanted to see the waterfalls in Yosemite National Park. There are eight major waterfalls that people visit. When it rains, many small waterfalls form. Yosemite Falls is the tallest waterfall in the United States. We took a tour and saw two large waterfalls. Vernal Falls and Nevada Falls are not as tall as Yosemite Falls. They are still amazing to see. We watched the water cascade down the sides of the mountains. We could see rainbows in the water. We even felt the mist of water from the falls as we walked by.

We also hiked through the Mariposa Grove. It is a forest filled with only very large trees. These trees are called sequoias. Many people think they are the biggest living things on our planet. They can grow to be over 200 feet tall. These trees are about 3,000 years old.

Wow! Look at how tall these trees are! They are also very old.

There are hotels in Yosemite National Park, but we camped in our tent.

My mom took this picture of Vernal Falls. Isn't the rainbow cool?

I heard people love to look at the mountains in the moonlight. Someday, when I am older, I will hike a mountain at night.

Hi Jay,
It looks like you had a really fun time. I can't wait to visit Yosemite again!
Talk to you soon,
Maria

August 11

We slept outside in our tent. The park has a campfire set up for visitors to use. We swam in a lake just as the sun was going down. Then we warmed up by sitting around the fire. We were tired from all the walking. We had seen many things for the first time on this trip. I had never seen rock climbers hanging off the side of a mountain! I had never seen waterfalls so high. I had never seen a forest filled with trees so tall.

When the sun went down we looked for the Moon. It was high in the sky. It was high above the peak of the tallest mountain in Yosemite. When I was in my tent at night, I imagined I could see Half Dome in the distance. This was a great vacation!

---

campfire a fire made outdoors by people who are camping

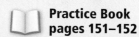
Practice Book
pages 151–152

Reading Strategy

Review and Retell

Go back and review the selection.

- Retell something Jay did on August 9.
- Retell something Jay did on August 10.

Think It Over

1 What was one place Jay visited?

2 Do you think Jay wants to try rock climbing? Why or why not?

3 How did Jay feel about his family vacation to Yosemite National Park?

301

Word Analysis & Fluency

Word Analysis

Greek and Latin Word Roots

Many English words come from Greek or Latin. For example, the word **circle** comes from the Latin root, **circ**. **Circ** means "round."

Half Dome is a mountain that looks like the top of a **circle.**

The Latin root in each word is in red.

animal   popular

cascade   vacation

Practice

Complete each statement.

1. The root *anim* means "life, spirit." So, an **animal** is ___.
   a. living   b. wild   c. tame

2. The root *vac* means "to be empty or free." During a **vacation,** you are likely to have ___.
   a. no time   b. free time   c. a good time

3. The root *popu* means "people." At a **popular** vacation spot, you're likely to see ___.
   a. plants   b. animals   c. people

4. The root *cas* means "fall." So, a **cascade** can be a ___.
   a. pool of water   b. water fountain   c. waterfall

Fluency

Read for Speed and Accuracy

You should read quickly. But never read so quickly that you lose your understanding.

Practice

| Read for one minute. | ▶ | Count the words you read. | ▶ | Study any hard words. | ▶ | Read and count again. |

We wanted to see the waterfalls in Yosemite National	9
Park. There are eight major waterfalls that people visit.	18
When it rains, many small waterfalls form. Yosemite Falls	27
is the tallest waterfall in the United States. We took a tour	39
and saw two large waterfalls. Vernal Falls and Nevada Falls	49
are not as tall as Yosemite Falls. They are still amazing to	61
see. We watched the water cascade down the sides of the	72
mountains. We could see rainbows in the water. We even	82
felt the mist of water from the falls as we walked by.	94
We also hiked through the Mariposa Grove. It is a forest	105
filled with only very large trees. These trees are called	115
sequoias. Many people think they are the biggest living	124
things on our planet. They can grow to be over 200 feet	136
tall! These trees are about 3,000 years old.	144

Comprehension

Review and Retell

What would you do if you wanted to tell a friend about this selection? You can review and retell it!

- When you **review**, you re-read the parts of the selection that tell the main points.
- When you **retell**, you tell the main points of the selection to someone else.

Learning Strategy

Retelling

Retell some of the highlights of Jay's trip to a partner.

? Ask your partner to respond to the Big Question for this reading.

Practice

Write two sentences that retell what happened on August 7.

August 7

On our first day we drove to Glacier Point. Our goal was to ascend to the very top. We had a great view from there. We saw a huge waterfall. We could see Yosemite Valley at the bottom. There were so many trees in the valley! We saw Half Dome mountain. It looks like the top of a circle. We passed rock climbers on the way down. People from all over the world come to climb rocks in Yosemite. It looked fun but also a little scary!

Practice Book page 154

Use a Main Idea and Details Chart

Reviewing the main idea and details in a selection will help you remember what you have read. Then you can write the main idea and details in a chart. You can use your chart to retell the selection to a partner.

Practice

Copy and complete this Main Idea and Details Chart. Go back and review parts of the text to help you.

```
                    ┌─────────────────────┐
                    │      Main Idea      │
                    │                     │
                    └─────────────────────┘
                     ↑        ↑        ↑
┌──────────────┐ ┌──────────────┐ ┌──────────────┐
│ Supporting   │ │ Supporting   │ │ Supporting   │
│ Detail       │ │ Detail       │ │ Detail       │
│              │ │              │ │              │
└──────────────┘ └──────────────┘ └──────────────┘
```

Extension

Write a brief description about something you really liked or disliked about a place you have visited. Discuss your description with a partner or group.

305

Grammar & Writing

Articles

The words *a*, *an*, and **the** are **articles**. **The** is a definite article because you use it before a specific noun, as in **the** blue dish. The words *a* and *an* are indefinite articles because they do not refer to a specific noun, as in *an* elephant.

Rule Box

Use *a* before nouns that begin with consonants; use *an* before nouns that begin with vowels or vowel sounds.

Words that begin with an *h* use *an* if they have a vowel sound: *an hour*.

Words that begin with a long *u* sound, use *a* because *u* actually sounds like yoo: *a uniform*.

Practice

Write the correct article(s) for each noun.

1. honor
2. book
3. Earth

4. horse
5. apple
6. boat

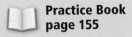
**Practice Book
page 155**

Write a Concluding Paragraph

A concluding paragraph ties the ideas from previous paragraphs together. Aya wrote a concluding paragraph about her vacation to Lake Sebago in her email to Carolina.

From: aya@ansonia.com
To: C_Mendez@workit.com
Subject: Our lake trip
Date: July 21

Hi Carolina,

We spent most of our days swimming, boating, and fishing. One day, we took a cruise around the entire lake and saw interesting birds and animals. We used the outdoor grill for dinner every night. My brother didn't catch any fish, so we ate hamburgers and corn on the cob. All in all, it was a great vacation. I hope we can come back next year.

See you soon,
Aya

SPELLING TIP

Keep a list in your notebook of words that you find hard to spell. Add to your list when you are reading or writing.

Practice Book page 156

Practice

Write an e-mail to a friend that summarizes a trip you took. Discuss your e-mail with a partner or group.

Writing Checklist

✓ Did you summarize your trip?

✓ Did you make it clear to your reader where you went?

✓ Did you give interesting details about your visit?

✓ Can a partner understand your e-mail?

Jay Writes a Research Paper

by Jay Rabin and Maria Reyes

From: Jay_Rabin@lincolnschool.net
To: mreyes@californianet.com
Date: June 5
Subject: What's up, Maria?

Hi Maria,

Not much is new in Pennsylvania. I can't wait for summer. We still have to finish the school year, though.

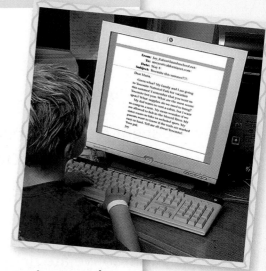

Jay has to write a research paper.

I just found out I have to write a research paper. Our teacher asked us to start thinking of topics. Because I'm going to Yosemite National Park this summer, I want to write about park rangers. Park rangers are important, and they have cool jobs. I think I want to become one!

Have you ever written a research paper? If so, what did you write about? Do you have any tips for me? I know research papers are an important kind of writing. I want to do a great job!

Write back soon if you can. My mom said she would take me to the library on Saturday.

Your friend,
Jay

Maria has some great ideas that will help Jay write his paper.

From: mreyes@californianet.com
To: Jay_Rabin@lincolnschool.net
Date: June 6
Subject: Re: What's up, Maria?

Hi, Jay,

Yes, I have written a research paper. It was about community recycling programs. I really learned a lot. Writing about park rangers is a great idea. But, it's a big topic. I think you should make your topic more specific. What interests you the most about park rangers? Write about that. Some good topics might be how to become a park ranger, what park rangers do, or even the history of park rangers.

You should make your topic more specific before you go to the library. Then you'll have an easier time finding information. When I started to research recycling, my topic was too big. I had a stack of books, magazines, and newspaper articles as tall as I am! So, I made my topic more specific: community recycling programs. Then, I needed only the books about my topic. Information about recycling cars or reusing plastic was interesting, but it was too much information for my paper.

Did your teacher say you could use Web sites as sources? If so, ask a librarian to help you find good information. I was amazed at the information we found online.

Your friend,
Maria

From: Jay_Rabin@lincolnschool.net
To: mreyes@californianet.com
Date: June 13
Subject: Research is fun

Hey Maria,

Thanks for the advice. My research is going well. In fact, I'm in the computer lab at the library right now!

The day after I got your message, our teacher talked to us about picking topics that aren't too big or too small. You were right!

I decided to write about what park rangers in Yosemite do. I found lots of books, magazine and newspaper articles, and references at the library. The Internet has lots of stuff too. It can be hard to tell which Web sites have correct information. Sometimes, people make up stuff and post it on the Internet. That's why I'm glad I worked with the librarian. If I look for more sites on the Internet while I'm home, I will ask my mom or dad to help me check them.

When I finish this message, I will start to take notes. It's nice and quiet here in the library. I can really concentrate! I'm going to find the best information, and then put it into my own words. I will write each idea on its own index card. I'm glad I have a big stack of cards!

Your pal,
Jay

From: mreyes@californianet.com
To: Jay_Rabin@lincolnschool.net
Date: June 14
Subject: Re: Research is fun

Hey Jay!

It's a great idea to put information in your own words. Also, I wrote the source on the back of each card to help keep track of my sources. List the title, author, publisher, and page or the Web site address. It may take more time, but it's worth it!

It will be helpful to reread your notecards when you are finished with your research. It's fun to put the note cards in order. They will make writing your outline much easier!

Your friend,
Maria

The library is a great place to find information about your topic. Remember to talk quietly.

Make sure to write down all of your sources and include them in your paper.

From: Jay_Rabin@lincolnschool.net
To: mreyes@californianet.com
Date: June 16
Subject: Rough draft time!

Hi again, Maria,

I got your message at the library. You helped me a lot!

I organized my note cards. But, I didn't have much information about what Yosemite park rangers do in the winter. So I did more research. After that, I wrote my outline. I included all the important ideas. This way, I didn't forget anything.

Then I wrote my rough draft! My teacher looked it over today. It didn't have many spelling or grammar mistakes because I read it a few times before I handed it in. My introduction was clear, and my body paragraphs were organized. My teacher said I need to work on my conclusion. She also reminded me to indent all my paragraphs. I'm going to work on that now. I'll also add my sources.

Do you know why we need sources and a bibliography?

Your friend,
Jay

From: mreyes@californianet.com
To: Jay_Rabin@lincolnschool.net
Date: June 20
Subject: Re: Rough draft time!

Hey Jay,

Wow! You sure did a lot of work on your research paper! Don't forget to send me a copy when you are finished.

You know what? I had the same problem with my rough draft. I didn't have a good conclusion. Then I remembered that conclusions sum up the important points from the body paragraphs. That's what I did. It was easy!

You remembered to put all your information in your own words, right? Well, even though you did that, you still have to show where you found the information. The bibliography is a list of the sources you used. It shows each source's title, author, and some other information. If you used a Web site, you include its address.

I'm sure you learned a lot about park rangers at Yosemite. Do you still want to be one someday?

Your friend,
Maria

The librarian can help you find books on your topic.

The Big Question

Why are national parks important?

Written	Oral	Visual/Active
Poem	**Conversation**	**Poster**
Write a poem about a park you have visited or about Jay's trip to Yosemite. Include details about the park and what people can do there for fun.	With a partner, talk about why national parks are important. Then talk with another pair of students.	Design a poster for a national park. Show tourists using the park in a variety of ways.
Brochure	**Debate**	**Bumper Sticker**
Create a brochure for a national park. Include information about its location, activities, and visiting hours. Illustrate your brochure with sketches or photos from the park's Web site.	Choose whether you would rather vacation at a national park or in a city. As teams, talk about the reasons for and against choosing each vacation spot.	Create a bumper sticker that tells about a national park and why people should visit it.
Newspaper Article	**Script**	**Blueprint**
Research and write a newspaper article about an event or activity that takes place at a national park.	Write a script a tour guide might use to show tourists around a national park. Be sure to include the park's most popular attractions.	Use your imagination to design a new national park. Draw a plan for the park that includes its features and activity areas.

✔ Learning Checklist

Word Analysis and Phonics

✔ Distinguish between *v* and *w* sounds.

✔ Identify variant vowel /oo/ sounds.

✔ Identify Latin word roots.

Comprehension

✔ Connect text to self.

✔ Use a 5W Chart.

✔ Draw conclusions.

✔ Use a KWL chart.

✔ Review and retell.

✔ Use a Main Idea and Details Chart.

Grammar and Writing

✔ Identify different types of sentences.

✔ Identify active and passive voice.

✔ Use articles correctly.

✔ Write a business letter.

✔ Write a paragraph in active voice.

✔ Write a concluding paragraph.

Self-Evaluation Questions

- What do you understand about national parks?

- How easy or difficult was doing research for you?

- What grade or score do you deserve on your research paper? Why?

315

Research Report

Writing a research report is an important skill. In a research report, you explain a topic you have studied in detail.

STEP 1: CHOOSE A TOPIC

The most important step in writing a research report is choosing a topic. Sometimes your teacher will give you the topic to research. Other times you will have to pick it yourself.

If you can choose your own topic, choose a topic you *want* to write about. Be careful that your topic is not too simple or too complicated. If it is, you will have too much, or too little, information to work with.

STEP 2: PREWRITE AND RESEARCH

After you choose your topic, you need to start your research. You can use a KWL chart to help you figure out what you already know about your topic and what you would like to learn.

You can ask the librarian to help you find information. The librarian can show you references, books, magazines, newspapers, and even Web sites! Ask an adult to check the Web sites you use for your research. You may even find people in your community to interview about your topic.

Write down all the information you find on your topic. Get a pack of index cards. Take organized notes on the cards. Make sure the notes are in your own words. Make sure you keep track of your sources. Write what you learn on one side of a card. Then write the source on the back of it. When you list the source, be sure to include the title, author, publisher, and page or Web site address.

STEP 3: OUTLINE

If you think you have enough information on your topic, it is time to write an outline. Read all of your index card notes. Set aside any information that you feel is not important.

Put your cards in an order that makes sense. Read your index cards again. Make sure you have all the information you need. Then use the cards to write an outline. The outline should show the ideas you will use in your paper. The ideas should be listed in the order you will write about them. Look at Elena's outline:

I. Why visit San Antonio?
   A. We want to visit all 50 states.
   B. Many fun things to see and do

II. What is special about the River Walk?
   A. walking
   B. boat rides

III. What historical places can I visit in San Antonio?
   A. The Alamo
   B. San Antonio Missions National Historical Park

IV. What other places can I see in San Antonio?
   A. Guinness Book of World Records
   B. Ripley's Haunted House

V. Conclusion
   A. Why I am going in the summer?
   B. What if it rains?

STEP 4: WRITE A DRAFT

Now you are ready to write your first draft. Your paper should start with an introduction. This tells your readers about your topic. Next comes the body of the paper. This has all the information that you researched. The body might be two paragraphs. It might be ten paragraphs. The length of your report will depend on how much research you have done. Finally, you will have a conclusion. This will summarize the topic for your reader. Look at an excerpt from Elena's first draft:

Elena Rodriguez
San Antonio, Texas

My mom and me want to visit all 50 states. We want to visit Texas next. My mom and I picked San Antonio as our spot for Texas. I am really excited to go there cuz it has some cool and fun things like very big water park, a Sea World, the River Walk, and the Alamo. San Antonio also has a zoo and some fun museums.

The River Walk is a place where you can walk or take a boat ride on the San Antonio River. A lot of people call it Paseo de Rio, which means River Walk. The officials city drain the river every January so they can clean the trash from the bottom. You can take a boat ride 35 minutes long. You can even get married there? There are also so many restaurants and stores, I can't wait to do some shopping.

San Antonio also history. The Alamo was a mission where a battle took place. The battle was between a Mexican dictater, Antonio Lopez de Santa Anna with his men and Travis William and his settlers. William Travis outnumbered 189 to 4000. The Alamo be very important to the independence of Texas. I seen pictures of the Alamo but I want to see in person. My mom and me might also visit Spanish missions at San Antonio Missions Park.

STEP 5: REVISE

After you have written your paper, read it carefully. Use the proofreading marks on page 342 to make any corrections. Look up any words you think you spelled incorrectly in the dictionary. Make sure that you have the correct names and dates in your paper. Add any details you may have forgotten. Ask yourself:

- Are the ideas presented in the best order?
- Is there a clear beginning, middle, and end?
- Does each paragraph have a main idea and supporting details?
- Did you cite your sources correctly?

Plagiarism

Plagiarism is presenting someone else's words, ideas, or work as your own. If the idea or words are not yours, be sure to give credit by citing the source in your work. Plagiarizing can result in your failing the assignment, or worse.

Ask a partner to read your writing and make comments about it. This is called a **peer review**. Decide what changes you want to make. Then rewrite your draft.

STEP 6: EDIT

This is the time to look at word choice, sentence fluency, and writing conventions. Reread your paper. Proofread for mistakes in spelling, grammar, and punctuation. Correct any mistakes you find.

When you edit and proofread your draft, use the editing marks on page 342 of the Writing Handbook to mark the changes.

Look at Elena's final version of her paper.

Elena Rodriguez
San Antonio, Texas

My mom and I want to visit all 50 states. We want to visit Texas next. We chose San Antonio for our Texas visit. I am really excited because it has some cool and fun things like the River Walk and the Alamo. San Antonio also has a zoo and some fun museums.

There is a River Walk in San Antonio. The River Walk is a place where you can walk or take a boat ride on the San Antonio River. A lot of people call it by its Spanish name, Paseo de Rio. The city officials drain the river every January so they can clean the trash from the bottom. You can take a boat ride that is 35 minutes long. There are so many restaurants and stores. I can't wait to do some shopping.

San Antonio also has a lot of history. The Alamo was a mission where a battle took place. The battle was between a Mexican dictator, Antonio Lopez de Santa Anna, with his men and William Travis and his settlers. The Alamo is very important to the independence of Texas. My mom and I might also visit Spanish missions at San Antonio Missions National Historical Park.

I think San Antonio, Texas, is going to be a good place to visit because it has lots of interesting and historic places to see. Mom and I will be going in the summer. Even if it rains I still think it will be fun because there are a few museums you can go to and other places like the Guinness Book of World Records and Ripley's Haunted House. I am looking forward to going. San Antonio is my kind of place.

Works cited:

San Antonio Riverwalk May 31, 2007
<www.longmancornerstone.com>

Travel Channel Destination Guides June 1, 2007
<www.longmancornerstone.com>

Convention and Visitors Bureau-San Antonio June 2, 2007
<www.longmancornerstone.com>

Kelly, Kate and Zeman, Anne. *Everything You Need to Know About American History Homework: A Desk Reference for Students and Parents.* New York, NY. Scholastic. 1997. p. 45.

STEP 7: PUBLISH

Once you have revised and proofread your paper, share it with others. Look at these publishing ideas.

- Post your paper on the bulletin board.
- Photocopy your paper. Hand it out to your classmates and family members.
- Attach it to an email and send it to friends.
- Send it to a school newspaper or magazine for possible publication.

Once you have shared your work with others, you may want to put it in your portfolio. A **portfolio** is a folder or envelope in which you keep your writing. If you keep your work in a portfolio, you can look at what you have written over a period of time. This will let you see if your writing is improving. It will help you become a better writer.

Most importantly, don't forget to congratulate yourself on a job well done!

Handbook

How to Learn Language

Learning a language involves listening, speaking, reading, and writing. You can use these tips to make the most of your language learning.

LISTENING

1. Listen with a purpose.
2. Listen actively.
3. Take notes.
4. Listen to speakers on the radio, television, and Internet.

SPEAKING

1. Think before you speak.
2. Speak appropriately for your audience.
3. Practice reading aloud to a partner.
4. Practice speaking with friends and family members.
5. Remember, it is okay to make mistakes.

READING

1. Read every day.
2. Use the visuals to help you figure out what words mean.
3. Reread parts that you do not understand.
4. Read many kinds of literature.
5. Ask for help.

WRITING

1. Write something every day.
2. Plan your writing before you begin.
3. Read what you write aloud. Ask yourself whether it makes sense.
4. Check for spelling and grammar mistakes.

How to Study

Here are some tips for developing good study habits.

- **Schedule a time for studying.** It is easier to develop good study habits if you set aside the same time every day to study. Once you have a study routine, it will be easier for you to find time to prepare for larger projects or tests.

- **Create a special place for studying.** Find a study area where you are comfortable and where you have everything you need for studying. If possible, choose an area that is away from telephones or television. You can play music if it helps you to concentrate.

- **Read the directions first.** Make sure you understand what you are supposed to do. Ask a partner or your teacher about anything you do not understand.

- **Preview the reading.** Look at the pictures, illustrations, and captions in the reading. They will help you understand the text.

- **Learn unfamiliar words.** Try to figure out what unfamiliar words mean by finding context clues in the reading. If you still can't figure out the meaning, use a dictionary.

- **Take notes.** Keep notes in a notebook or journal of important things you want to remember from the reading.

- **Ask questions.** Write any questions you have from the reading. Discuss them with a partner or your teacher.

How to Build Vocabulary

Use these ideas to help you remember the meanings of new words.

Keep a Vocabulary Notebook Keep a notebook of vocabulary words and their definitions. Test yourself by covering either the word or the definition.

Make Flashcards On the front of an index card, write a word you want to remember. On the back, write the meaning. Use the cards to review the words with a partner or family member.

Say the Words Aloud Use your new words in sentences. Say the sentences to a partner or a family member.

How to Use a Book

The Title Page The title page states the title, the author, and the publisher.

The Table of Contents The table of contents is at the front of a book. The page on which a chapter begins is next to its name.

The Glossary The glossary is a small dictionary at the back of a book. It will tell you the meaning of a word, and sometimes how to pronounce it. Use the glossary the same way you would use a dictionary.

The Index The index is at the back of a book. It lists subjects and names that are in the book, along with page numbers where you can find information.

The Bibliography The bibliography at the back of a book or chapter lets you know the books or sources where an author got information.

How to Use a Dictionary and Thesaurus

The Dictionary

You can find the **spelling**, **pronunciation**, **part of speech**, and **definitions** of words in the dictionary.

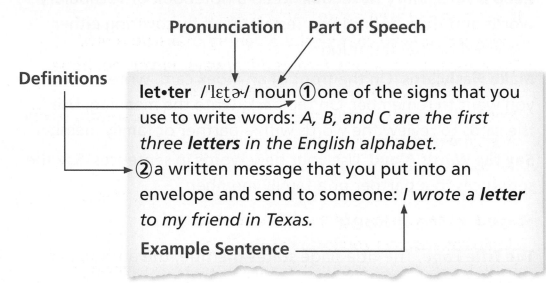

Pronunciation   Part of Speech

Definitions

let•ter /ˈlɛt̬ər/ noun ① one of the signs that you use to write words: *A, B, and C are the first three **letters** in the English alphabet.*

② a written message that you put into an envelope and send to someone: *I wrote a **letter** to my friend in Texas.*

Example Sentence

The Thesaurus

A thesaurus is a specialized dictionary that lists **synonyms**, or words with similar meanings, and **antonyms**, or words with opposite meanings. Words in a thesaurus are arranged alphabetically. You can look up the word just as you would look it up in a dictionary.

Main entry: sad
Part of speech: adjective[1]
Definition: unhappy
Synonyms: bitter, depressed, despairing, down, downcast, gloomy, glum, heartbroken, low, melancholy, morose, pessimistic, sorry, troubled, weeping
Antonyms: cheerful, happy

How to Take Tests

Taking tests is part of going to school. Use these tips to help you answer the kinds of questions you often see on tests.

True-False Questions

- If a statement seems true, make sure it is *all* true.
- The word *not* can change the meaning of a statement.
- Pay attention to words such as *all*, *always*, *never*, *no*, *none*, and *only*. They often make a statement false.
- Words such as *generally*, *much*, *many*, *sometimes*, and *usually* often make a statement true.

Multiple Choice Questions

- Try to answer the question before reading the choices. If your answer is one of the choices, choose it.
- Eliminate answers you know are wrong.
- Don't change your answer unless you know it is wrong.

Matching Questions

- Count each group to see whether any items will be left over.
- Read all the items before you start matching.
- Match the items you know first.

Fill-In-the-Blank Questions or Completions

- Read the question or incomplete sentence carefully.
- Look for clues in the question or sentence that might help you figure out the answer.
- If you are given possible answers, cross each out as you use it.

Short Answers and Essays

- Take a few minutes to organize your thoughts.
- Give only the information that is asked for.
- Answer as clearly as possible.
- Leave time to proofread your response or essay.

How to Read Maps and Diagrams

Informational texts often use maps, diagrams, graphs, and charts. These tools help illustrate and explain the topic.

Maps

Maps show the location of places such as countries, states, and cities. They can also show where mountains, rivers, lakes, and streets are located. A compass rose on the map shows which way is north. A scale shows how miles or kilometers are represented on the map.

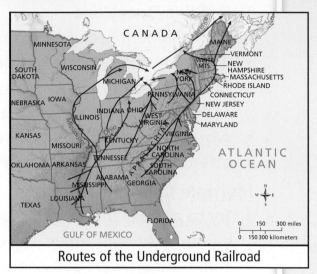

Routes of the Underground Railroad

Diagrams

Diagrams are drawings that explain things or show how things work. Some diagrams show pictures of how objects look on the outside or on the inside. Others show the different steps in a process.

This diagram shows the steps of the Scientific Method. It helps you understand the order and importance of each step.

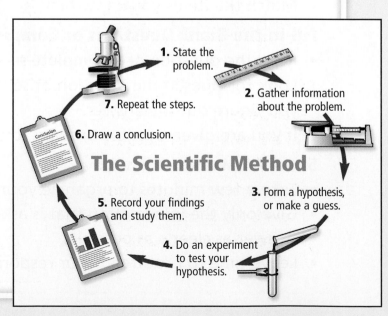

1. State the problem.
2. Gather information about the problem.
3. Form a hypothesis, or make a guess.
4. Do an experiment to test your hypothesis.
5. Record your findings and study them.
6. Draw a conclusion.
7. Repeat the steps.

The Scientific Method

How to Read Graphs

Graphs show how two or more kinds of information are related or alike. Three common kinds of graphs are **line graphs**, **bar graphs**, and **circle graphs**.

Line Graph

A **line graph** shows how information changes over a period of time. This line graph explains how the Native American population of Central Mexico changed over 120 years.

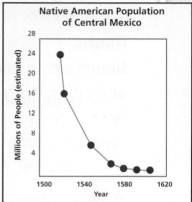

Bar Graphs

We use **bar graphs** to compare information. For example, this bar graph compares the populations of the 13 United States in 1790.

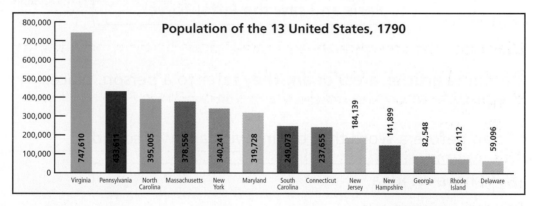

Circle Graphs

A **circle graph** is sometimes called a pie chart because it looks like a pie cut into slices. Circle graphs are used to show how different parts of a whole compare to each other.

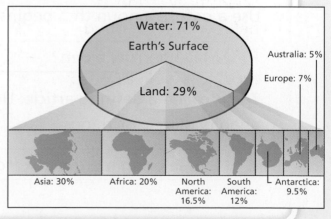

329

Parts of Speech

In English there are nine **parts of speech**: nouns, articles, pronouns, verbs, adjectives, adverbs, prepositions, conjunctions, and interjections.

Nouns

Nouns name people, places, or things.

A **common noun** is a general person, place, or thing.

person	thing	place
The **student** brings a **notebook** to **class**.

A **proper noun** is a specific person, place, or thing.

person	place	thing
Joe went to **Paris** and saw the **Eiffel Tower**.

Articles

Indefinite articles are *a* or *an*. They refer to a person, place, or thing.

Use *an* before a word that begins with a vowel sound.

I have **an** idea.

Use *a* before a noun that begins with a consonant sound.

May I borrow **a** pen?

The is called a **definite article**. Use *the* to talk about specific people, places, or things.

Please bring me **the** box from your room.

Pronouns

Pronouns are words that take the place of nouns or proper nouns.

proper noun	pronoun
Ana is not home. **She** is babysitting.	

	Subject Pronouns	**Object Pronouns**
Singular	I, you, he, she, it	me, you, him, her, it
Plural	we, you, they	us, you, them

A **subject pronoun** replaces the subject of a sentence. A **subject** is who or what a sentence is about.

subject	subject pronoun (singular)
Dan is a student. **He** goes to school every day.	

Object pronouns replace a noun or proper noun that is the object of a verb. An **object** receives the action of a verb.

object	object pronoun (singular)
Lauren gave **Ed** the notes. Lauren gave **him** the notes.	

Possessive pronouns replace nouns or proper nouns. They show who owns something.

	Possessive Pronouns
Singular	mine, yours, hers, his
Plural	ours, yours, theirs

Verbs

Verbs express an action or a state of being.

An **action verb** tells what someone or something does or did.

Verbs That Tell Actions You Can See	Verbs That Tell Actions You Cannot See
dance swim	know sense

A **linking verb** shows no action. It links the subject with another word that describes the subject.

Examples of Linking Verbs		
look	smell	is
are	appear	seem

A helping verb comes before the main verb. They add to a verb's meaning.

	Helping Verbs
Forms of the verb *be*	am, was, is, were, are
Forms of the verb *do*	do, did, does
Forms of the verb *have*	have, had, has
Other helping verbs	can, must, could, have (to), should, may, will, would

Adjectives

Adjectives describe nouns. An adjective usually comes before the noun it describes.

> **tall** grass   **big** truck

An adjective can come *after* the noun it describes. This happens in these kinds of sentences.

> The bag is **heavy**. The books are **new**.

Adverbs

Adverbs describe the action of verbs. They tell *how* an action happens. Adverbs answer the question *Where?, When?, How?, How much?,* or *How often?*

Many adverbs end in *-ly*.

> easily   slowly

Some adverbs do not end in *-ly*.

> seldom   fast   very

In this sentence, the adverb *everywhere* modifies the verb *looked*. It answers the question *Where?*

>   verb   adverb
> Nicole looked **everywhere** for her book.

Prepositions

Prepositions show time, place, and direction.

Time	Place	Direction
after	above	across
before	below	down

In this sentence, the preposition *above* shows where the bird flew. It shows place.

> preposition
> A bird flew **above** my head.

In this sentence, the preposition *across* shows direction.

> preposition
> The children walked **across** the street.

A **prepositional phrase** starts with a preposition and ends with a noun or pronoun. In this sentence, the preposition is *near* and the noun is *school*.

> ┌ prepositional phrase ┐
> The library is **near the new school**.

Conjunctions

A **conjunction** joins words, groups of words, and whole sentences. Common conjunctions include *and*, *but*, and *or*.

The conjunction *and* joins two proper nouns: *Allison* and *Teresa*.

> proper   proper
> noun   noun
> Allison **and** Teresa are in school.

The conjunction *or* joins two prepositional phrases: *to the movies* and *to the mall*.

> prepositional   prepositional
> phrase   phrase
> They want to go to the movies **or** to the mall.

The conjunction *but* joins two independent clauses.

> independent clause   independent clause
> Alana baked the cookies, **but** Eric made the lemonade.

Interjections

Interjections are words or phrases that express emotion.

Interjections that express strong emotion are followed by an exclamation point.

> **Wow!** Did you see that catch?

A comma follows interjections that express mild emotion.

> **Gee,** I'm sorry that your team lost.

Sentences

Clauses

Clauses are groups of words with a subject and a verb.

- An **independent clause** can stand on its own as a complete sentence.
- A **dependent clause** cannot stand alone as a complete sentence.

Sentences

A simple sentence is an independent clause. It has a subject and a verb.

> subject   verb
> The dog barked.

A **compound sentence** is made up of two or more simple sentences, or independent clauses.

> ┌────── independent clause ──────┐   ┌── independent clause ──┐
> The band has a lead singer, **but** it needs a drummer.

Sentence Types

Declarative sentences are statements. They end with a period.

> We are going to the beach on Saturday.

Interrogative sentences are questions. They end with a question mark.

> Will you come with us?

Imperative sentences are commands. They end with a period or an exclamation point.

> Put on your life jacket. Now jump in the water!

Exclamatory sentences express strong feeling. They end with an exclamation point.

> I swam all the way from the boat to the shore!

Punctuation

End Marks

End marks come at the end of sentences. There are three kinds of end marks: periods, question marks, and exclamation points.

Periods

- Use a period to end a statement (declarative sentence).
- Use a period to end a command or request (imperative sentence).
- Use a period after a person's initial or abbreviated title.
- Use a period after abbreviations.

Question Marks and Exclamation Points

- Use an exclamation point to express strong feelings.
- Use a question mark at the end of a question.

Commas

Commas separate parts of a sentence or phrase.

- Use a comma to separate two independent clauses linked by a conjunction.
- Use commas to separate the parts in a series. A series is a group of three or more words, phrases, or clauses.
- Use a comma to set off introductory words or phrases.
- Use commas to set off an interrupting word or phrase.
- Use a comma to set off a speaker's quoted words.
- Use commas to set off the name of the person being addressed in a letter or speech.

Semicolons and Colons

Semicolons can connect two independent clauses. Use them when the clauses are closely related in meaning or structure.

Colons introduce a list of items or important information. Also use a colon to separate hours and minutes when writing the time.

Quotation Marks

Quotation marks set off direct quotations, dialogue, and some titles.

- Commas and periods always go inside quotation marks.
- If a question mark or exclamation point is not part of the quotation, it goes outside the quotation marks.
- Use quotation marks to set off what people say in a dialogue.
- Use quotation marks around the titles of short works of writing.

Apostrophes

Apostrophes can be used with singular and plural nouns to show ownership or possession. To form the possessive, follow these rules:

- For singular nouns, add an apostrophe and an *s*.
- For singular nouns that end in *s*, add an apostrophe and an *s*.
- For plural nouns that do not end in *s*, add an apostrophe and an *s*.
- For plural nouns that end in *s*, add an apostrophe.
- Apostrophes are also used in contractions, to show where a letter or letters have been taken away.

Capitalization

There are five main reasons to use capital letters:

- to begin a sentence
- to write the pronoun *I*
- to write the names of proper nouns
- to write a person's title
- to write the title of a work (artwork, written work)

Modes of Writing

Narration is used to tell a story. Here are some types of narration.

- Autobiography is the story of a person's life, told by the writer.
- Biography is the story of a person's life told by another person.
- A short story is a short, fictional narrative.

Exposition gives information or explains something. Here are some types of exposition.

- Compare and Contrast writing analyzes the similarities and differences between two or more things.
- Cause and Effect writing explains why something happened and what happens as a result.
- Problem and Solution writing describes a problem and offers one or more solutions to it.
- How-To writing explains how to do or make something.
- Description paints a picture of a person, place, thing, or event.

Persuasion is writing that tries to convince people to think or act in a certain way.

Functional writing is writing for real-world uses. Here are some types of functional writing.

- You might fill out a form to sign up for lessons, take a field trip, or apply for a library card.
- You might create an invitation to a holiday party.

The Writing Process

The writing process is a series of steps that helps you write clearly.

Step 1: Pre-write

When you pre-write, you explore ideas and choose a topic. You identify your audience, and you choose your purpose for writing.

To choose a topic, try one or more of these strategies.
- **List** many ideas that you might want to write about.
- **Freewrite** about some ideas for five minutes.
- **Brainstorm** a list of ideas with a partner.

To identify your audience, think about who will read your writing. What do they already know? What do you need to explain?

To identify your purpose for writing, ask:
- Do I want to entertain my audience?
- Do I want to inform my audience?
- Do I want to persuade my audience?

Now, decide on the best form for your writing. Gather and organize the details that will support your topic.

Step 2: Draft

You start writing in this step. Put your ideas into sentences. Put your sentences into paragraphs. Begin to put your paragraphs in order. Don't worry too much about grammar and spelling. You will have a chance to correct any errors later.

Step 3: Revise

This is the time to look at your ideas and the organization of your writing. Read your first draft. Ask yourself:

- Are the ideas presented in the best order?
- Is there a clear beginning, middle, and end?
- Does each paragraph have a main idea and supporting details?

Ask a partner to read your writing and make comments about it. This is called a peer review. Decide what changes you want to make. Then rewrite your draft.

Step 4: Edit/Proofread

This is the time to look at word choice, sentence fluency, and writing conventions. Reread your paper. Proofread for mistakes in spelling, grammar, and punctuation. Correct any mistakes you find.

When you edit and proofread your draft, use these proofreading marks to mark the changes.

Editing/Proofreading Marks		
To:	Use This Mark:	Example:
add something	∧	We ate rice, bean*s*, and corn.
delete something	ℯ	We ate rice, beans, and corns.
start a new paragraph	¶	¶ We ate rice, beans, and corn.
add a comma	⸜	We ate rice, beans and corn.
add a period	⊙	We ate rice, beans, and corn⊙
switch letters or words	∼	We ate rice, baens, and corn.
change to a capital letter	<u>a</u>	we ate rice, beans, and corn.
change to a lowercase letter	A̸	WE ate rice, beans, and corn.

Proofreading Checklist

- Check your spelling. Look up words you aren't sure of in the dictionary.
- Check your grammar and usage. Use the Grammar Handbook to help you correct sentences.
- Review capitalization and punctuation. Make sure each sentence begins with a capital letter and uses proper end punctuation.

Step 5: Publish

Once you have revised and proofread your paper, share it with others. Look at these publishing ideas.

- Post your paper on the bulletin board.
- Photocopy your paper. Hand it out to your classmates and family members.
- Attach it to an email and send it to friends.
- Send it to a school newspaper or magazine for possible publication.

Once you have shared your work with others, you may want to put it in your portfolio. A portfolio is a folder or envelope in which you keep your writing. If you keep your work in a portfolio, you can look at what you have written over a period of time. This will let you see if your writing is improving. It will help you become a better writer.

Build Your Portfolio

You may want to keep your completed writing in your portfolio. It is a good idea to keep your drafts, too. Keep comments you receive from your teacher or writing partner, as well.

Reflect on Your Writing

Make notes on your writing in a journal. Write how you felt about what you wrote. Use these questions to help you get started.

- What new things did you learn about your topic?
- What helped you organize the details in your writing?
- What helped you revise your writing?
- What did you learn about yourself as you wrote?

Rubric for Writing

A rubric is a tool that helps you assess, or evaluate, your work. This rubric shows specific details for you to think about when you write. The scale ranges from 4 to 1, with 4 being the highest score and 1 being the lowest.

4	Writing is clearly focused on the task. Writing is well organized. Ideas follow a logical order. Main idea is fully developed and supported with details. Sentence structure is varied. Writing is free of fragments. There are no errors in writing conventions.
3	Writing is focused, with some unnecessary information. There is clear organization, with some ideas out of order. The main idea is supported, but development is uneven. Sentence structure is mostly varied, with some fragments. Writing conventions are generally followed.
2	Writing is related to the task but lacks focus. Organization is not clear. Ideas do not fit well together. There is little or no support for the main idea. No variation in sentence structure. Fragments occur often. Frequent errors in writing conventions.
1	The writing is generally unfocused. There is little organization or development. There is no clear main idea. Sentence structure is unvaried. There are many fragments. Many errors in writing conventions and spelling.

Writing and Research

Sometimes when you write, you need to do research to learn more information about your topic. You can do research in the library, on the Internet, and by viewing or listening to information media.

Library Reference

Encyclopedias contain basic facts, background information, and suggestions for additional research.

Biographical references provide brief life histories of famous people in many different fields.

Almanacs contain facts and statistics about many subjects, including government, world history, geography, entertainment, business, and sports.

Periodicals are past editions of magazines. Use a periodical index to find articles on your topic.

Vertical files contain pamphlets on a wide variety of topics.

Electronic databases provide quick access to information on many topics.

Citing Sources

When you do research, you read what other people wrote. The material you research is called the source or reference. When you tell who wrote the material, this is called citing the source. It is important to cite each source you use when you write.

In your paper, note each place in which you use a source. At the end of the paper, provide a list that gives details about all your sources. A bibliography and a works cited list are two types of source lists.

- A **bibliography** provides a listing of all the material you used during your research.

- A **works cited list** shows the sources you have quoted in your paper.

Plagiarism

Plagiarism is presenting someone else's words, ideas, or work as your own. If the idea or words are not yours, be sure to give credit by citing the source in your work. It is a serious offense to plagiarize.

Look at the chart of the Modern Language Association (MLA). Use this format for citing sources. This is the most common format for papers written by middle and high school students, as well as college students.

MLA Style for Listing Sources

Book	Pyles, Thomas. *The Origins and Development of the English Language*. 2nd ed. New York: Harcourt Brace Jovanovich, Inc., 1971.
Signed article in a magazine	Gustaitis, Joseph. "The Sticky History of Chewing Gum." *American History* Oct. 1998: 30–38.
Filmstrips, slide programs, videocassettes, DVDs	*The Diary of Anne Frank*. Dir. George Stevens. Perf. Millie Perkins, Shelly Winters, Joseph Schildkraut, Lou Jacobi, and Richard Beymer. Twentieth Century Fox, 1959.
Internet	*National Association of Chewing Gum Manufacturers*. 19 Dec. 1999. <http://www.longmancornerstone.com> [Indicate the date you found the information.]
Newspaper	Thurow, Roger. "South Africans Who Fought for Sanctions Now Scrap for Investors." *Wall Street Journal* 11 Feb. 2000.
Personal interview	Smith, Jane. Personal interview. 10 Feb. 2000.

Internet Research

The Internet is an international network of computers. The World Wide Web is a part of the Internet that lets you find and read information.

To do research on the Internet, you need to open a search engine. Type in a keyword on the search engine page. **Keywords** are words or phrases on the topic you want to learn about. For example, if you are looking for information about your favorite musical group, you might use the band's name as a keyword.

To choose a keyword, write a list of all the words you are considering. Then choose a few of the most important words.

Tips

- Spell the keywords correctly.
- Use the most important keyword first, followed by the less important ones.
- Open the pages at the top of the list first. These will usually be the most useful sources.

How to Evaluate Information from the Internet

When you do research on the Internet, you need to be sure the information is correct. Use the checklist to decide if you can trust the information on a Web site.

✔ Look at the address bar. A URL that ends in "edu" is connected to a school or university. A URL that ends in "gov" means it is a site posted by a state or federal government. These sites should have correct information.

✔ Check that the people who write or are quoted on the site are experts, not just people telling their ideas or opinions.

✔ Check that the site is free of grammatical and spelling errors. This is often a hint that the site was carefully designed and researched.

✔ Check that the site is not trying to sell a product or persuade people.

✔ If you are not sure about using a site as a source, ask an adult.

Information Media

Media is all the organizations that provide news and information for the public. Media includes television, radio, and newspapers. This chart describes several forms of information media.

Types of Information Media	
Television News Program	• Covers current news events • Gives information objectively
Documentary	• Focuses on one topic of social interest • Sometimes expresses controversial opinions
Television Newsmagazine	• Covers a variety of topics • Entertains and informs
Radio Talk Show	• Covers some current events • Offers a place for people to express opinions
Newspaper Article	• Covers one current event • Gives details and background about the event
Commercial	• Presents products, people, or ideas • Persuades people to buy or take action

How to Evaluate Information from Various Media

Because the media presents large amounts of information, it is important to learn how to analyze this information. Some media sources try to make you think a certain way instead of giving you all the facts. Use these techniques to figure out whether you can trust information from the media.

✔ Sort facts from opinions. A fact is a statement that can be proven true. An opinion is how someone feels or thinks about something. Make sure any opinions are supported by facts.

✔ Be aware of the kind of media you are watching, reading, or listening to. Is it news or a documentary? Is it a commercial? What is its purpose?

✔ Watch out for bias. **Bias** is when the source gives information from only one point of view. Try to gather information from several points of view.

✔ Discuss what you learn from different media with your classmates or teachers. This will help you determine if you can trust the information.

✔ Read the entire article or watch the whole program before reaching a conclusion. Then, develop your own views on the issues, people, and information presented.

▣ How To Use Technology in Writing

Writing on a Computer

You can write using a word processing program. This will help you when you follow the steps in the Writing Process.

- When you write your first draft, save it as a document.
- As you type or revise, you can move words and sentences using the cut, copy, and paste commands.
- When you proofread, you can use the grammar and spell check functions to help you check your work.

Keeping a Portfolio

Create folders to save your writing in. For example, a folder labeled "Writing Projects—September" can contain all of the writing you do during that month.

Save all the drafts of each paper you write.

Computer Tips

- Rename each of your revised drafts using the SAVE AS function. For example, if your first draft is "Cats," name the second draft "Cats2."
- If you share your computer, create a folder for only your work.
- Always back up your portfolio on a server or a CD.

Glossary

A

accompany go with (p. 233)

adapt change to fit a new situation (p. 167)

adversary person you are fighting or competing against (p. 112)

alpine in or related to the Alps or other high mountains (p. 282)

area part of a place (p. 271)

arena large building used for sports and entertainment (p. 76)

ascend move higher (p. 296)

assess decide how good or significant something is (p. 63)

assist help someone (p. 233)

assistance help or support (p. 194)

attitude point of view; state of mind (p. 37)

authorities people who are in charge of an area (p. 195)

B

biome community of plants, animals, and insects–like a rain forest or a desert (p. 166)

blister swelling on a surface (p. 86)

bore carried something (p. 62)

broad wide (p. 86)

C

carry take something somewhere (p. 36)

cascade small waterfall (p. 296)

charge run toward something quickly (p. 36)

chased ran after someone or something (p. 76)

classify put into groups (p. 167)

cliffs areas of high steep rock (p. 270)

clumsy moving awkwardly (p. 8)

cobblestone small round stone set in the ground to make a street (p. 126)

code words, letters, or numbers used to send secret messages (p. 232)

colonies countries that are controlled by other countries (p. 112)

comment talk about; say something about (p. 297)

compensate make payment (p. 113)

complete whole; with nothing left out (p. 8)

353

complexity complicated or detailed (p. 245)

conduct lead or direct (p. 9)

confidential not intended to be shown or told to other people (p. 126)

conservation saving or protecting of animals or plants (p. 282)

consume eat or use something (p. 183)

contained held something inside (p. 86)

context situation, events, or information related to something (p. 221)

contract legal agreement (p. 113)

convention formal meeting for a specific purpose (p. 139)

cooperate work together with someone else to get something done (p. 62)

correspond write messages to someone (p. 296)

cottage small house in the country (p. 36)

courageous brave (p. 22)

criminal someone who has done something wrong and is punished by the law (p. 76)

crown special hat made of gold and jewels worn by a king or queen (p. 112)

curious wanting to know or learn about something (p. 126)

damage harm something (p. 194)

debate public talk at which people give opinions about a subject (p. 139)

delegates people who are chosen to speak, vote, and make decisions for a group (p. 126)

demonstrate show how to do something (p. 221)

desert large area of land where it is hot and dry (p. 166)

distinct separate; different from others (p. 87)

ecosystem all the animals and plants in a particular area (p. 282)

emergency unexpected and dangerous situation (p. 22)

environment world of land, sea, and air that you live in (p. 282)

equator imaginary line around the middle of Earth (p. 166)

error mistake (p. 63)

escape get out of a place (p. 232)

establish start a company, system, situation, etc. (p. 195)

evaluate look at a situation carefully (p. 23)

exclaimed said something loud and suddenly because you were surprised (p. 8)

features traits or characteristics (p. 283)

federal relating to the central government of a country that controls a group of states (p. 138)

flea market market, usually in the street, where old or used goods are sold (p. 244)

forest area where there are a lot of trees (p. 296)

goal something you want to achieve (p. 183)

grasslands large areas of land covered with wild grass (p. 166)

grateful thankful (p. 62)

grove piece of land with trees growing on it (p. 270)

handle hold or touch something (p. 194)

harmonies combinations of musical notes that sound good together (p. 244)

hearing ability to hear (p. 220)

important very useful or valuable (p. 8)

improve become better, or make something better (p. 8)

improvisation something done without any preparation (p. 244)

individual separate from others in the same group (p. 127)

instruments objects used for making music (p. 220)

interact act upon or with another (p.87)

intervene try to stop an argument, problem, or war (p. 22)

item single piece or thing (p. 37)

355

K

kazoo simple musical instrument that you play by holding it to your lips and making sounds into it (p. 244)

L

landmarks things that help you recognize where you are, such as a famous building (p. 232)

landslide sudden falling of a lot of soil and rocks down the side of a hill, cliff, or mountain (p. 282)

legal allowed by law (p. 127)

legislature institution that has the power to make or change laws (p. 138)

liberty freedom (p. 112)

M

marvelous very good (p. 62)

meadow field with wild grass and flowers (p. 296)

merchants people who buy and sell large quantities of goods (p. 126)

merry happy and having fun (p.86)

midst in the middle of something (p. 86)

migrated moved from one place to another (p. 182)

millet plant like grass with small seeds that are used for food (p. 62)

motive underlying reason for doing something (p. 77)

musicians people who play musical instruments very well (p. 220)

N

national parks large areas of land throughout the United States that the government has set aside for nature (p. 270)

O

ocean very large area of water (p. 166)

orphan child or animal without parents (p. 182)

P

peak pointed top of a hill or mountain (p. 296)

peeked quickly looked at something (p. 36)

percussion drums and other musical instruments which you play by hitting or shaking them (p. 220)

pods family group of marine animals (p. 182)

predator animal that kills and eats other animals (p. 182)

principle rule or idea that you believe is right and that makes you behave in a particular way (p. 77)

privy bathroom or outhouse (p. 126)

project plan or activity (p. 9)

R

refugees people who have to leave their own countries, especially because of war (p. 22)

region area or location (p. 271)

relief assistance in time of difficulty (p. 194)

representation having someone speak, vote, or make decisions for you (p. 112)

republic a government with an elected head of state (p. 138)

reunite come together again (p. 182)

rhythms strong patterns of sound (p. 244)

riverbank land on the sides of a river (p. 232)

S

scarce not enough of something (p. 36)

scenic beautiful views of nature (p. 282)

secluded private and quiet (p. 282)

secrecy keeping information secret (p. 126)

secret idea or plan that you do not tell other people about (p. 232)

separate not connected to each other; apart (p. 138)

sequoias very tall trees that grow near the coast in Oregon and California (p. 270)

share have or use something together with other people (p. 36)

sounds things that you hear (p. 220)

specific precise; exact (p. 283)

startle make someone suddenly surprised or shocked (p. 86)

starvation suffering or death from lack of food (p. 182)

357

stranded needing help because you cannot move from a particular place (p. 194)

surrender stop fighting because you know you cannot win (p. 138)

suspicious not willing to trust someone or something (p. 8)

swollen became larger because of injury or sickness (p. 76)

tailors people whose job is to make suits, coats, etc. (p. 126)

task job or piece of work that must be done (p. 23)

taxes money you must pay to the government (p. 112)

teamwork ability of a group to work well together, or the effort the group makes (p. 22)

tracks marks made on the ground by an animal, person, or vehicle (p. 232)

training process of being taught how to do a particular job (p. 22)

tributaries rivers or streams that flow into a larger river (p. 270)

tropical coming from the hottest and wettest part of the world (p. 166)

tundra large flat lands in northern areas where it is very cold and there are no trees (p. 166)

valley area of lower land between two lines of hills or mountains (p. 296)

variety differences within something (p. 245)

veteran someone who has been a soldier in a war (p. 138)

vibrations continuous shaky movements (p. 220)

virtue good quality of someone's character (p. 62)

wander move or travel with no particular purpose (p. 76)

Index

361

Credits

ILLUSTRATORS: Meredith Johnson 10–16, **Julie Downing** 38–43 **Soud** 64–69 **TK** 92 **Gary Torrisi** 100–103 **Doris Ettlinger** 153–157 **middle Richard Ward** 166 **Jennifer Emery** 258–261.

COVER: Terry Kovalcik

ICONS: Bill Melvin

LETTER LOGOS: Jan Bryan-Hunt

UNIT 1: 2–3 TK; 5 top ©Dana White/PhotoEdit Inc.; 5 upper middle ©Steve Gorton/ Dorling Kindersley; 5 lower middle PhotoEdit Inc.; 5 bottom ©David Young-Wolff/ PhotoEdit Inc.; 6 left top © Mark Richards/PhotoEdit Inc.; 6 left bottom ©Tony Freeman/ PhotoEdit Inc.; 6 right top © Danilo Balducci/Peter Arnold; Inc.; 6 right bottom ©David Young-Wolff/PhotoEdit Inc.; 7 left top © Cindy Miller Hopkins/Danita Delimont Photography; 7 left bottom © Michele Molinari/ Danita Delimont Photography; 7 right bottom © Demetrio Carrasco/Stone Allstock/Getty Images; 7 right top © Michael Dunning/ Photo Researchers Inc; 8 top © Jonathan Nourok/PhotoEdit Inc.; 8 middle; Managed Photographs; 8 bottom © Jeff Greenberg/PhotoEdit Inc.; 9 top © Donna Day/ Stone Allstock/Getty Images; 9 middle © Vicky Kasala Productions/Image Bank/Getty Images; 9 bottom Masterfile; 17 © Cleo Photography/ PhotoEdit Inc.; 18 Alami Images; 19 © Frank Siteman/Omni-Photo Communications Inc.; 20 Will Hart; 21 Bettman/CORBIS; 22 top © Dwayne Newton/PhotoEdit Inc.; 22 bottom © Vince Streano/NY/CORBIS; 23 top © Blair M. Seitz Creative Eye/MIRA.com; 23 right © Bill Aron/PhotoEdit Inc.; 23 bottom AP World Wide Photos; page 24 MSF Sygma/CORBIS; 25 Kieran Doherty/Reuters/CORBIS;26 Philippe Desmazes/ Getty Images; 27 Robert Harding World Imagery; 28 top © Ton Koene/Peter Arnold Inc.; 28 bottom left © Keren Su National Geographic Image Collection; 28 bottom right ©Hoang Dinh Nam/ Getty Images; 29 top Liason/Getty Images; 29 bottom Ian Berry/Magnum Photos; 30 National Geographic Image Collection; 31 Liason/Getty Images; 32 © Antonia Reeve/Photo Researchers Inc.; 33 © Patrick Robert Sygma/CORBIS; 34 © Jimin Lai/Getty Images; 35 © Jorgen Schytte/ Peter Arnold Inc.; 36 top © Don Mason/CORBIS; 36 middle Taxi/Getty Images; 36 bottom © G. Baden Gerhard Steiner/CORBIS; 37 top National Geographic Image Collection; 37 right © Nelly Boyd/Robert Harding World Imagery; 37 bottom © Martin Harvey/Peter Arnold Inc.; 44 © David Young-Wolff/PhotoEdit Inc.; 45 © Clive Streeter/ Dorling Kindersley; 46 © Ralph Talmont/Aurora and Quanta Productions; 47 © Jerry Mason/Photo Researchers Inc.; 48 © Robert E. Daemmrich/Stone Allstock/Getty Images; 50 © Al Grillo/AP World Wide Photos; 52–53 © Clark J. Mishler/Creative Eye/Mira.com

UNIT 2: 56–57 Anton Vengo/Superstock; 59 top © Dave King/Dorling Kindersley; 59 upper middle © Annabella Bluesky/Photo Researchers Inc.; 59 middle © Mark Richards/ PhotoEdit Inc.; 59 bottom PhotoEdit Inc.; 60 top left © A. Ramey/Stock Boston; 60 bottom left ©Ellen Sensei 60 top right Ryan's Well Foundation; 60 bottom right;© Mark Richards/PhotoEdit Inc.; 61 top left Victor Englebert; 61 bottom left © Claire Liembach/ Robert Harding World Imagery; 61 top right Picture Desk/Kobal Collection; 61 bottom right © David Young-Wolff/PhotoEdit Inc.; 62 top © David Young-Wolff/PhotoEdit Inc.; 62 middle © Peter Anderson/Dorling Kindersley; 62 bottom © Richard Morrell/CORBIS; 63 top © Charlotte Thege/Peter Arnold Inc.; 63 middle © Gary Ombler/Dorling Kindersley; 63 bottom Lawrence Migdale; 70 Dorling Kindersley; 71 © Betty Press/Woodfin Camp and Associates; 72 © Christopher and Sally Gable/Dorling Kindersley; 73 © Chad Ehlers/ Stock Connection; 74 © Kristin Mosher/Danita Delimont Photography; 75 © Roger de la Harpe/Dorling Kindersley; 76 top © Peter Blackwell Nature Picture Library; 76 bottom © Susan Van Etten/PhotoEdit Inc.; 77 top © David Shale Nature Picture Library; 77 middle © Chad Ehlers Stock Connection; 77 bottom © John Boykin/PhotoEdit Inc.; 78–79 Hulton Archive/ Getty Images; 80 CORBIS; 81 Hulton Deutsch/ CORBIS; 82 Hulton Archive/Getty Images; 83 Hulton Archive/Getty Images; 84 Hulton Archive/ Getty Images; 85 Canali Photobank; 86 top National Geographic Image Collection; 86 middle © Peter Reali CORBIS; 86 bottom Stockbyte/ Getty Images; 87 top © David Lok Superstock Inc.; 87 right © Stewart Cohen/Photo Library.

com; 87 bottom right © Jane Burton/Dorling Kindersley; 89 (background) Bettman/CORBIS; 89 (inset) © Cinema Photo/CORBIS; 90 © Arni Katz/PhotoLibrary.com; 91 Library of Congress; 92 © Donna Day Stone/Allstock/Getty Images; 93 Picture Desk Inc./Kobal Collection; 94 CORBIS; 95 Bettman/CORBIS; 96 Picture Desk Inc./ Kobal Collection; 97 Photofest; 98 content.answers.com; 99 Everett Collection

UNIT 3: 106–107 The Granger Collection; 109 top © Jeff Greenberg/PhotoEdit Inc. 109 top middle © Tony Perottet/Ambient Images; 109 middle © Steve Gorton/Dorling Kindersley; 109 bottom © Ahmad Masood/Reuters America/CORBIS; 110 top left © Martin Beebe/CORBIS; 110 bottom left EMG Education Management Group; 110 top right © Greg Johnston/Danita Delimont Photography; 110 bottom right © Patricia Jordan/ Peter Arnold Inc.; 111 top left © Joseph Nettis/ Photo Researchers Inc.; 111 bottom left Pearson Learning Photo Studio; 111 top right © Mark Antman/The Image Works; 111 bottom right © Steve Gorton/Dorling Kindersley; 112 top right © Atsuko Tanaka/ CORBIS; 112 middle right © Ron Bell/AP World Wide Photos; 112 bottom CORBIS; 113 top © Mark C. Burnett/Photo Researchers Inc. 113 top right © Michael John O'Neill/ Image Bank/Getty Images; 113 bottom © Mike Theiler Bettman/CORBIS; 114 Bettman/CORBIS; 115 Pearson Education Modern Curriculum; 116 Bettman/CORBIS; 117 The Granger Collection; 118 top AP World Wide Photos; 118 bottom left Bettman/CORBIS; 118 right © Najlah Feanny Bettman/CORBIS; Bettman/CORBIS; 119 top left Hulton Archive/Getty Images; 119 top right AP World Wide Photos; 119 center AP World Wide Photos; 119 bottom AP World Wide Photos; 120 The Granger Collection; 121 Viesti Associates; 122 Library of Congress; 123 The Granger Collection; 124 The Anne S.K. Military Collection; 125 © Lisa Poole/AP World Wide Photos; 126 top right Architect of the Capitol; 126 right; Stockbyte/ Getty Images; 126 bottom left © David Mager/ Pearson Learning Photo Studio; 126 bottom National Geographic Image Collection; 127 top © Robert Fried Photography; 127 top right © Michelle D. Bridwell/ PhotoEdit Inc. Inc.; 127 middle right © Tony Souter Dorling Kindersley; 127 bottom © Mark Johnson/Creative Eye/MIRA.

com; 128 The Granger Collection NY © Eduardo Garcia/Getty Images; 129 The Granger Collection NY © Eduardo Garcia/Getty Images; 130 The Granger Collection NY © Eduardo Garcia/Getty Images;131 Independence National Historical Park; 132 © Cary Wolinsky/Aurora & Quanta Productions Inc.; 133 Hulton Archive/Getty Images; 134 William H. Sadler; 135 Metropolitan Museum of Art; 136 © David Merewether/Dorling Kindersley; 137 Hulton Archive/Getty Images; 138 top right Photodisc/Getty Images; 138 right © Paul Conklin/PhotoEdit Inc.; 138 bottom left Art Resource NY; 139 middle right © Jeff Greenberg/ PhotoEdit Inc.; 140 Library of Congress; 141Bridgeman Art Library International; 142 New York Historical Society; 143 Hulton Archive/Getty Images; 144 Photo Researchers Inc.; 145 Hulton Archive/Getty Images; 146 © Les Riess/Omni-Photo Communications; 147 © Mary Steinbacher/ PhotoEdit Inc.; 148 © Joe Sohm/The Stock Connection; 149 © Paul Conklin/ PhotoEdit Inc. ; 150 Hulton Archive/Getty Images; 151 PhotoEdit Inc.

UNIT 4: 160–161 Felicia Martinez/Photoedit Inc. 163 top © Bill Bachman/Creative Eye/MIRA.com; 163 top middle Omni-Photo Communications Inc. 163 middle © David Noton/Nature Picture Library; 163 bottom left © Jose B. Ruiz/Nature Picture Library; 163 bottom right © Charlotte Thege/Peter Arnold Inc.; 164 top left The Image Works; 164 bottom left © Esben/Anderson/Omni-Photo Communications Inc. 164 top right © Mark Edwards/Peter Arnold Inc. 164 bottom right © Adam Buchanan/Danita Delimont Photography; 165 top left © Yva Momatiuk/Stock Boston; 165 bottom left © Eascott-Momatiuk/The Image Works; 165 top right © Pete Oxford/Nature Picture Library; 165 bottom right Ellen Sinisi; 166 top © David Parker Photo Researchers Inc.; 166 middle right © Ben Osborne/Nature Picture Library; 166 bottom © Chad Ehlers/The Stock Connection; 167 top © David Noton/Nature Picture Library; 167 middle right © Glen Allison Photodisc/Getty Images; 167 bottom © Dave Fleetham Pacific Stock; 168–169 © Barbara Nelson Creative Eye/MIRA.com; 169 (inset)© Pete Oxford/Nature Picture Library; 170 top National Geographic Image Collection; 170 bottom © Marc Bernardi/The Stock Connection; 171